Mum's Christmas present
1983; alas unsigned.

D1101286

MEMORABLE MUNROS

Memorable Munros

*A diary of ascents of the
highest peaks in Scotland*

RICHARD GILBERT

Richard Gilbert

DIADEM BOOKS · LONDON

Father Alban Crossley
Ampleforth Abbey
York YO6 4EN

First published privately in 1976 (paperback)

Reprinted in 1978 (paperback)

Second edition (in hardback) 1983 by
Diadem Books Limited, London

All trade enquiries to:
Cordee, 3a De Montfort Street, Leicester

British Library Cataloguing in Publication Data

Gilbert, Richard, 1937 Nov. 17
    Memorable Munros.
    1. Walking – Scotland – Highlands
    2. Highlands (Scotland) – Description and travel
    I. Title
    796.5'22   GV199.44.G72S27

ISBN 0 906371 41 4

Production for the publisher by
Chambers Green Ltd., Tunbridge Wells, Kent

Printed in Great Britain by Biddles of Guildford

CONTENTS

Maps in the Text

Introduction

The Munros

The Munros are the separate mountains over 3,000ft in Scotland. The list was compiled in 1891 by Sir Hugh Munro after much patient research. At that time his knowledge of the topography of the Highlands was probably second to none. The list was published in the 1891 edition of the Scottish Mountaineering Club Journal, Sir Hugh being a founder member of the club. At once the 'Munros' provided a framework for hill walkers and the pursuit of Munro bagging began.

Sir Hugh's first list consisted of 283 separate mountains, but resurveying has demoted some and has also thrown up three extra mountains making 279 in all. There has been much discussion since the list was first published as to what constitutes a 'separate' mountain, but until 1981 the Scottish Mountaineering Club agreed that Sir Hugh's judgement and list shall stand

I think it is most unlikely that a list of the 1,000 metre (3,282ft) peaks would replace the Munros. It would have no tradition and many excellent peaks, just gaining their places as Munros, would be lost.

Sir Hugh climbed all the mountains on his list except two, and those walkers and climbers who strive to follow his footsteps are called Munroists.

The Munros: A Note for the Second Edition

Since the first edition of Memorable Munros was

7

published in 1976 there has been another revision of Munro's Tables.

Periodic revisions have taken place ever since Sir Hugh Munro's first list was published in the 1891 edition of the Scottish Mountaineering Club Journal. Sir Hugh's first list contained 283 separate mountains but a few years after the original list was published the O.S. produced revised six-inch maps of Scotland and these threw up many discrepancies.

Sir Hugh at once started a revision of his list and he collected together a file of notes and he established a card index of the individual mountains. Unfortunately Sir Hugh died before his own, revised, list could be published but J. R. Young, A. W. Peacock and helpers from the SMC prepared revised tables in 1921, basing the revisions on Sir Hugh's notes and card index. The 1921 list contained 276 separate mountains.

In 1933 it was suggested that a systematic revision of Munro's Tables should be undertaken. A small committee was set up by the SMC to look into the matter and they reported that Munro's Tables was too much of an historical document to alter and the only changes made to the 1921 edition should be corrections of proved errors. Thus the inclusion of Beinn Tarsuinn (after several independent surveys had made it over 3,000ft) raised the number of Munros to 277.

More recent surveys have discovered three more separate peaks over 3,000ft, Beinn a'Chlaidheimh, Ruadh Stac Mor and Sgurr nan Ceannaichean, while one Munro from the old list (Beinn an Lochain) has been found wanting in height and has been deleted. This should give a total of 279 separate Munros.

But to my bitter disappointment the new edition of Munro's Tables, published in 1981 by the SMT, contains a quite arbitrary revision of the accepted list by its editors Hamish Brown and J. C. Donaldson. Their final total of Munros is 276 because they have taken the liberty of elevating to separate Munro status the four peaks of Sgor an Iubhair, Garbh Chioch Mhor, Mullach an Rathain (Liathach) and Sgurr Fiona (An Teallach) while demoting seven peaks in the Cairngorms and the Monadh Liath. These changes have not been made on grounds of height but solely at the whim of the editors.

Once we start tampering with the list of Munros we will never stop. To my knowledge no-one agrees with the Brown/Donaldson revisions and I find them incomprehensible. Poor Munro would turn in his grave if he knew that Carn Cloich-mhuillinn was no longer a separate mountain; this peak was the one he chose to leave until last because it was near his home and convenient for a final Munro party.

If Munro considered the great peaks of Liathach and An Teallach to be worthy of just one separate mountain entry in his list then so be it. Now they have each been given two summit entries, why? On the other hand the editors have left Beinn Eighe as a single entry which indicates inconsistency and what about Sgurr na Lapaich of Mam Sodhail, a separate peak if ever there was one?

My point is that the 1921 revised list should be sacrosanct except for changes indicated by re-surveys – the conclusion arrived at by the 1933 committee.

I do implore the SMT to rescind their unfortunate 1981 edition of Munro's Tables, a book which does not even list the spot height of the Munros in feet, the unit which was the basis of Sir Hugh's original list!

For the reasons given above I shall acknowledge, in

Memorable Munros, a total of 279 separate mountains.

Twelve years have passed since I first completed the ascent of the mountains on Munro's incomparable list. I still go to Scotland at every opportunity but some of the pressure and urgency has been removed from my mountain days. I move more slowly and, like A. E. Robertson the first Munroist, enjoy leisurely lunches basking beside cairns, weather permitting.

New surveys, with sophisticated equipment, keep throwing up new Munros and this keeps self-satisfied Munroists from complete idleness. It is really asking too much of us, sitting smugly in our armchairs beside the fire, to put on our boots again, drive to the Highlands and, with creaking joints, knock off another pimple. But we will go. Munro will be watching us, for the ghost of the Great Man stalks every cairn.

Notes about the Book
The purpose of this book is to provide armchair reading for fellow Munroists and temptation for those hill walkers and climbers not yet smitten with the remote tops of the Highlands.

The book is a personal account of the Scottish Munros and what they have meant to me rather than a detailed guide book. I have given some background information on early hill-walking in Scotland and on Sir Hugh Munro in particular, for one's thoughts automatically turn to the great man when one is on the hills, and his presence can be felt on every summit. His attitude and example have been a great inspiration to me. Remote mountains and bad weather were merely extra challenges to him, and if walking companions could not be found he would go alone.

The circuit was first completed in 1901 by the Reverend A. E. Robertson, and I have included some stories about him too.

I am often asked why Munroists pursue their mountains across miles of peat hag and bog, through rain, snow and mist. I cannot give a simple answer to this question but I hope this book will give the uninitiated something of an idea of the motivation behind the driving force.

Perhaps, above all, it was the four-day expedition round Loch Mullardoch in March 1962 while I was at University that made me realise the pleasures of winter mountaineering in Scotland. Carrying tents and food increases the safety factor enormously as well as providing the enjoyment of high camps. Trying to reach the summits of Munros provides extra impetus and ensures that the principal mountain areas of Scotland are covered.

Doing the Munros becomes a way of life. It is not only the time spent actually on the mountains, but also the build up to a week-end or holiday in Scotland. The packing of rucksacks, buying of food, choosing the objectives. In my case, time was always short and I would drive to Scotland overnight to save a day and to avoid the traffic. After driving many tens of thousands of miles, the transport cafes, the wait at Queensferry and Ballachulish before the bridges were built, the bends on the A82 alongside Loch Lomond and the rain drumming on the windscreen all became familiar, and made up part of the total experience.

One possible advantage in doing the Munros from a distance is that having driven a long way and having made complicated arrangements to get time off to be in the Highlands, one is very loath to waste a day. I always considered it worth starting out whatever the weather. On many occasions the day started very depressingly with rain and low cloud, only for it to clear later and provide the contrast that is essential for the Highland experience. Sometimes of course, conditions deteriorate and gaining one's Munro becomes a real fight against the elements. However unpleasant the day, in the evening one is consoled by the thought that there is one less mountain to do and the day has not been wasted festering in the tent. There is a feeling of achievement and well-being.

After the first three chapters which deal with the early munroists, I have started the list of my own ascents with my final Munro, Bidean nam Bian. Thereafter the mountains are grouped by region, the most northerly first. The date of my first ascent of a Munro being denoted in italics at the start of each account. I have then included any interesting information from later ascents.

The diaries have always been written up immediately after making an ascent and, on some of the expeditions, I have written the account in the tent before going to sleep.

Not all the ascents have been interesting and I have sometimes been a trifle dismissive in my account. It should be stressed, however, that certain Munros that I have found tedious due to bad weather or poor conditions, could provide magnificent climbs on better days.

RICHARD GILBERT
Crayke, York, 1983

CHAPTER 1

The Early Days

In the eighteenth century an English Officer stationed in the Highlands wrote home, 'Scotland is a wild and mountainous country inhabited by a barbarous people; there are nine months of winter, three of spring and no summer at all.'

It was against a background like this that Dr. Johnson and Boswell set out on their remarkable journey through the Highlands to the Hebrides in 1773. The success of the book published in 1785 made people aware for the first time of the warmth and hospitality of the Highlanders and the possibilities of travel to this remote part of Britain.

Earlier in the century, the country was opened up by the network of communications and excellent roads built by General Wade. He built the Fort William to Inverness road, the Dunkeld to Inverness road and the spectacular road, now a footpath, through the Corrieyairack Pass from Fort Augustus to Dalwhinnie.

In spite of the rapidly improving road network and the springing up of inns in the Highlands following the 1745 Rebellion, exploration of the remote hills and glens did not follow for many years. The fresh air and the beauty of the hills which bring the tourists to Scotland nowadays were looked upon with distaste in the eighteenth century. E. Burt in the 1720s wrote of the Highland hills: 'They are a dismal gloomy brown drawing upon a dirty purple and are most of all disagreeable when the heather is in bloom. The clearer the day, the more rude and offensive they are to the sight.' Even Dr. Johnson wrote of the hills: 'The appearance is that of matter incapable of form or usefulness, dismissed by Nature from her care and disinherited of her favours, left in its original elemental state or quickened only with one sullen power of useless vegetation.'

Mountains were climbed for professional rather than aesthetic reasons; by surveyors, sportsmen, geologists, meteorologists and soldiers. In 1880 and 1881 Clement Wragge, a meteorologist, ascended Ben Nevis every day from June 1 to November 1 without missing a single day. He would rise at 4 a.m., reach the summit at 9 a.m., make observations for two hours and return home by 3 p.m. He stopped when the permanently staffed Observatory was built.

The first recorded tourist ascent of Ben Lomond was in 1758, but by the end of the century ascents by men, women and foreigners were commonplace.

The more difficult ascents came much later, particularly on Skye. The Cuillins were regarded as exceptionally difficult. Sgurr nan Gillean was first climbed in 1836 by Professor Forbes, the Inaccessible Pinnacle in 1880 by Charles and Lawrence Pilkington and the Cioch in 1906 by Professor Norman Collie.

The Highlands started to be appreciated for their beauty in the nineteenth century and Queen Victoria had a very special place for them in her heart.

William IV and George IV had paid brief visits to Edinburgh but then twenty years elapsed before Queen Victoria in 1842, aged 23 and with two children and expecting a third, asked Sir Robert Peel to arrange a royal visit to Scotland. She travelled in the Royal Yacht because, on land, Peel feared for her safety from the Chartists.

Queen Victoria and Prince Albert were quite delighted with Scotland and they returned again in 1844. This time they journeyed to Blair Atholl and they explored Glen Tilt, the pass of Killiecrankie and the Falls of Bruar. On returning to England she wrote: 'The English coast appeared terribly flat. Lord Aberdeen was quite touched when I told him I was so attached to the dear, dear Highlands and missed the fine hills so much.'

In 1848 Queen Victoria and Prince Albert decided to have a royal residence on Deeside and they took the lease of Balmoral Castle. This location was recommended by Sir James Clarke on account of the climate, for the Queen was suffering mildly from rheumatic pains. The royal association with Deeside started from this time, for so taken with the area was the Queen, that a new Balmoral was built and the castle and estate were completed by 1859. Prince Albert set an excellent example to the area by his treatment of the estate workers. Prior to the royal arrival, the crofters lived in stone and mud bothies thatched with heather and the floors were of earth. The Prince housed the workers decently at moderate rent and he built new lodges for the keepers.

Over the next few years Queen Victoria energetically explored the Highlands from her summer residence at Balmoral. The Prince engaged in sporting activities. Together they ascended Ben Macdui, Lochnagar, Beinn a' Bhuird and Carn an Tuirc. Their experiences on these climbs were very similar to those met with

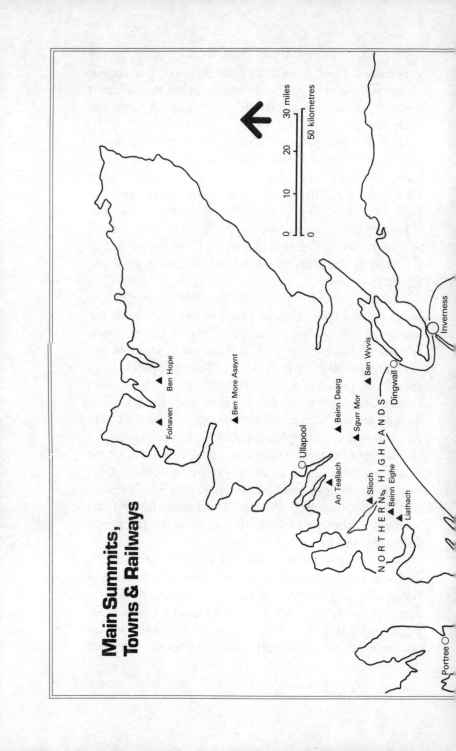

Main Summits, Towns & Railways

Foinaven ▲

Ben Hope ▲

Ben More Assynt ▲

An Teallach ▲

Sgurr Mor ▲

Beinn Dearg ▲

Ben Wyvis ▲

Ullapool ○

Slioch ▲

Beinn Eighe ▲
Liathach ▲

N O R T H E R N   H I G H L A N D S

Dingwall ○

Inverness ○

Portree ○

0   10   20   30 miles

0   50 kilometres

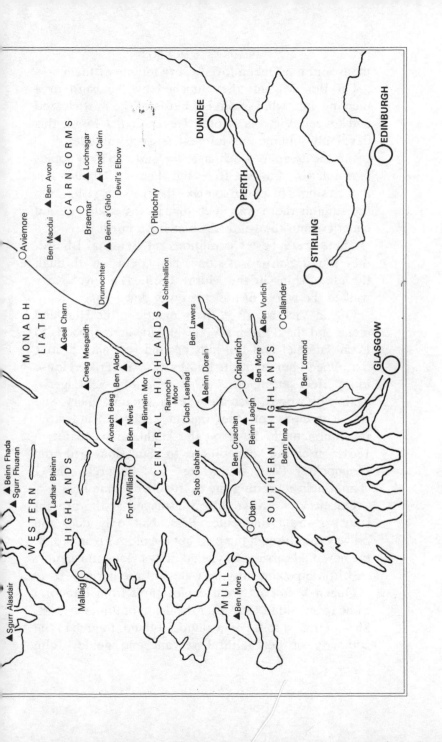

today and the Queen loved every minute of them.

On Ben Macdui they lunched by the cairn in a piercing cold wind and mist, but later the mist cleared and Queen Victoria wrote: 'Never shall I forget this day; truly sublime and impressive; such solitude.'

For the ascent of Lochnagar the party on their ponies assembled at Balloch Buie and 'Faithful Highlanders moved stones in a burn to make the crossing easier.' On the summit there was thick fog, it was cold, wet and cheerless and the wind was blowing a hurricane.

There were better conditions on Beinn a' Bhuird, they found Cairngorm stones and could see, through the glass, ships in the Moray Firth. The royal party walked the whole of the steep way down.

Queen Victoria loved the romantic in the Highland scene and the 'Queen's View' looking across woods to Loch Tummel and the hills beyond was named after her. One of her favourite houses was Ardverikie House in a perfect setting on the west shore of Loch Laggan, again with woods, loch and wild mountain scenery. She was conscious of the impact that the industrial revolution might have on the Highland scene for in 1861, after an expedition to Speyside and the Drumochter Pass, she wrote: '. . . So pretty but I cannot help regretting the railroad will come near.'

Queen Victoria would be dismayed at the present state of the Drumochter Pass. Not only does the railway run through the pass but the old A9 trunk road, the new dual carriageway, electricity pylons and an ugly cast iron pipe carrying the waters of the burn.

Queen Victoria's great explorations from Balmoral came to an end in 1861 after the death of Prince Albert. She continued to travel around Scotland, though in the company of her faithful servant and guide, John

Brown. The rumours that were circulated in England about her friendship with Brown were probably a result of jealousy in that the Queen was known to prefer the company of Scotsmen to that of Englishmen.

The Queen enjoyed Balmoral right up until her last visit in 1900. She encouraged her grandchildren to accompany her there and she still made regular visits to the local cottages where she had many friends.

CHAPTER 2

Sir Hugh Munro, Bart.

Hugh Thomas Munro was born in London in 1856. At the age of seventeen he was sent to Stuttgart to learn German and he started climbing in the Alps. His career was typical of a man from an upper-class background at that time. He was ADC to General Fielding and he went to South Africa as private secretary to the Governor of Natal. He was well known on the London scene as a magnificent dancer. After the Basuto War he returned to Scotland and managed the family estates at Lindertis in Fife for his father, Sir Campbell Munro. He stood as Conservative candidate for Kircaldy, but was not elected.

Sir Hugh was associated with the Scottish Mountaineering Club at its foundation and he almost never failed to attend a Club Meet or the Annual Dinner. He said on his election to President of the SMC in 1894 that he held the honour in higher esteem than if he had been made Prime Minister of Great Britain. He was also a member of the Alpine Club and a Fellow of the Royal Geographical Society.

As an after-dinner speaker he was inclined to be heavy and long winded and he liked to make his opinions known. When requested, at a dinner, to give a recitation he rose to his feet and said he wished to say a few words first. He proceeded to do so at great length.

From his many contributions to the journal of the SMC it can be seen that Sir Hugh had a particular liking for the Scottish hills in winter time. His days were always long and he was loath to waste a minute of them. He once set out for the hills late at night after a dinner, rather than risk missing an hour of daylight by a late start in the morning.

He would make long detours from the agreed route, leaving his companions and striding away, aneroid in hand, to investigate and make notes on remote summits.

In spite of his systematic analysis of the mountains and the energy he put into this, he remained something of a romantic. The distant views, clearing of the weather and the changing colours of the seasons delighted him.

The big estates and deer forests were thriving in Sir Hugh's time. He knew personally many of the Lairds and it was always possible for him to stay in the shooting lodges and bothies that abounded.

By the courtesy of the Marquis of Zetland, parties could enjoy the excellent hospitality of Mr. and Mrs. Angus at Larachantivore in Strathnasheallag. The suspension bridge outside the cottage was being used as early as 1910. Recommended too, was the old lodge of Benula Forest at Luib-na-damph west of Loch Mullardoch. This was a two-storey house served by a carriage road from Invercannich, but now both road and lodge are under the waters of Loch Mullardoch. The head keeper would send a man as guide for parties traversing Mam Sodhail and Carn Eige and he would also provide ponies. One could stay with Mrs. Scott at Alltbeithe cottage in Glen Affric and then cross the hills to Mrs. Finlayson's at Ben Ula Lodge.

Sir Hugh was often transported by his man in a 'dogcart' to the base of the mountains. Later he bought one of the first motor cars and the roads were sufficiently good for him to drive around, even to places as remote as Kinlochhourn.

Hotels were comparatively cheap. In 1904 complete board including packed lunch, afternoon tea and bath was five shillings and six pence at Kingshouse Hotel on Rannoch Moor and eight shillings at the Sligachan Hotel on Skye.

Munro's writings best portray the attitude he had towards the mountains and his remarkable determination and energy:

February 1880   Glas Maol range on a day of sun and hard frost. Views extending to the Campsie Fells 70 miles away.

1889   To Knoydart. At Inverie the Laird, Mr. Baird, met the steamer and would not let him stay at the inn but put him up at the Lodge. He walked over to Skiary on Loch Hourn and stayed at the beehive crofters cottage being fed on oatmeal, codling and bad whisky. The next day he lunched at Glenquoich Lodge with Mr. Malcolm the Factor, who drove him to Fort Augustus for the night. Then to Drumnadrochit by steamer, through Glen Urquhart to Invercannich and another night at Guisachan. The next day he walked over Sgurr na Lapaich and Mam Sodhail past the Falls of Glomach to Shiel Inn. From Shiel he did Sgurr Fhuaran and Sgurr na Carnach before crossing Mam Ratagan and Ben Sgriol to Glenelg where he embarked on the "Clansman' for Glasgow.

1890   Together with J. G. Stott, Munro searched for

the Cairnwell in dense fog, cold wind and lashing rain. At the end of the day they were met at Spital of Glenshee by Munro's man in the dog cart with dry clothes.

January 1890   Munro was alone on the Carn Liath range in deep powder snow which was raised in columns 100ft high by the high wind. The snow penetrated everything, filling his pockets and drifting between his shirt and waistcoat, where it melted and froze into a solid wedge of ice. Back home they had to scrape him down with a knife to get the frozen snow off.

March 1890   A solo walk by Munro from Dalwhinnie, he was able to cross the burns on the ice. He traversed the Aonach Beag, Beinn Eibhinn ridge and noted that mountains as remote as these were still cairned. He was back in Dalwhinnie after a fourteen-hour day in deep snow all the time. The following day he climbed Bheinn Bheoil and Ben Alder in a blizzard descending via Benalder Lodge to Loch Rannoch-side where he obtained lodgings.

May 1891   From Dalwhinnie again he climbed Sron Garbh, Mullach Coire an Iubhair, Creag Pitridh and Beinn a' Chlachair remarking on a small line of cairns leading to the summit of the last named mountain. These are still there. He complained of 'villainous peat hags' on the way back via Loch Pattack.

The next day he was on Ben Alder and actually had a ten-minute stop for a smoke on the summit.

He also climbed Beinn Dearg near Blair Atholl and, although he found it uninteresting, he thought it was one of the best viewpoints he had ever visited. On that occasion he could see sixty miles to the Saddle, Mam Sodhail, Ben Starav, the Cairngorms and Mull.

February 1892   Munro recorded a semaphore at the top of the Sgoran Dubh crags to signal the whereabouts of deer to the bothy by Loch Einich.

On February 9, he left Lynwilg Inn at 8.45 a.m. much regretting the late start(!) He ascended Cairngorm and Ben Macdui in dense freezing mist. A navigational error led him to descend towards Loch Avon instead of Loch Etchachan. It was now after sunset but he retraced his steps and made another attempt to find the correct route but this ended above cliffs and it was not until 5.45 p.m. that he reached Loch Etchachan. In darkness he reached Derry Lodge at 8.30 p.m., where he was entertained by the head stalker and his wife. Munro blamed the late start for his trouble but his fitness and reserves gave him a good margin of safety.

1898   On New Year's Day Munro was on Ben Nevis; it was a perfect frosty winter's day and he enjoyed the hospitality of the Observatory staff. The Observatory provided a useful telegraph service, for two days later when Inglis-Clark and Gibson were late off a climb, only a telegram wired from there to Fort William stopped a search party setting out.

1898   Munro wrote: 'Who has not regretted the hour lost in the morning?' Accordingly, he set out in the afternoon and cycled to Spital of Glenshee from Lindertis. He started walking at 11.00 p.m., noting the wind and snow were the reverse of the Irishman's statement: 'There was not much wind, but what there was blew very hard.' In poor weather Munro walked over Carn a' Gheoidh, Carn Bhinnein, Carn an Righ,

Beinn Iutharn Beag, An Socach and Socach Mor, returning home by 8.00 p.m. the following evening.

March 1900 Munro was in the North-West Highlands and he climbed A'Mhaighdean. It took him nearly six hours walking from Kinlochewe and he wrote: 'Few if any mountains are more difficult of access than A'Mhaighdean.'

While staying at the Aultguish Inn he had two disastrous days which lost him his reputation.

On the first day he left the Inn after lunch for Am Faochagach but the snow needed a lot of step-cutting and coming down Strath Vaich he was unable to cross a stream and had to detour to a keeper's house. He then mounted a horse but still arrived back at the Inn after midnight.

A day later in the company of H. Lawson he climbed Beinn Liath Mhor Fannaich, Sgurr Mor, Sgurr nan Clach Geala and Sgurr nan Each. While they were descending north towards Loch a' Bhraoin they had difficulty fording a stream and became benighted. For light they had precisely three matches. The first showed the map to be folded upside down, the second blew out and the third gave them insufficient information. After freezing and blundering about all night they reached the road at 7 a.m. to find Munro's driver still waiting with a fire alight and hot cocoa ready.

They did one other ascent from Aultguish. This was Beinn Dearg where they witnessed an enormous snow avalanche, over 100 yards across.

1904 Munro was a very regular member at Scottish Mountaineering Club Meets and he liked to arrive a day early to have a solitary day getting the feel of the hills and assessing the conditions. Before the 1904 Easter Meet he cycled from Aviemore to Loch Einich, and climbed Sron na Lairig in a ferocious blizzard exceeding anything he had ever experienced. Watchers by the shore of Loch an Eilein timed the spray being blown from one end of the Loch to the other at 100 m.p.h.

1906 Munro was on his way to Skye when he arrived one evening at Strathcarron Station. By night he did a lone twelve-hour traverse of Bidein a' Choire Sheasgaich and Lurg Mhor.

At that time the SMC members used to hire a guide for their climbs in Skye; he was John MacKenzie and was in great demand. Munro was apprehensive on rock and he was disappointed to find that MacKenzie had been permanently engaged by the Reverend A. E. Robertson who was staying at Sligachan. However, Munro tackled Sgurr nan Eag by night and was rewarded by a perfect dawn giving hot sun on the tops and a sea of cloud below 1,500ft. The Cuillin summits projected like islands and out to sea he could see the Hebrides from Barra Head to Harris.

Later that week Robertson offered Munro the services of Mackenzie and together they ascended the Pinnacle Ridge of Sgurr nan Gillean.

1908 To Skye again, but the unfortunate Munro could not secure John MacKenzie. He contented himself with the traverse of Sgurr na Banachdich and Sgurr Thormaid, and he also climbed Blaven, seeing St. Kilda from the top.

In July, Munro and a companion, W. Garden, made a night ascent of An Sgarsoch. They walked up Glen Tilt to the Memorial Bridge in heavy rain, finding the rivers Tilt and Tarf in high flood. They reached An Sgarsoch's cairn at 1.05 a.m. in thick mist, but their matches were wet and they could read neither map nor compass. Much to Munro's distress, for he had not climbed it, they abandoned Carn an Fhidleir and, knowing the wind was from the north, they were able to descend to the Geldie. The bridge at Geldie Lodge had been swept away and they had to make a long detour to cross the bridge at the junction of the Tarf and Bynack. They reached Linn of Dee at 8.10 a.m., both agreeing that An Sgarsoch was very uninteresting and not worth the ascent.

Munro recommended the Temperance Inn at Inverie as a centre for exploring Knoydart. He travelled by motor and he climbed Sgurr na Ciche and Sgurr nan Coireachan from Banchaolie on the Kinlochhourn road, returning via Kinlochquoich on a day of mist and rain.

In the Great War, Munro was past military age but he worked for the Red Cross in Malta. Later, with his two daughters, he opened a canteen for French troops at Tarascon in France. He caught pneumonia and died after a week's illness.

Of the mountains on his list, Munro had missed the Inaccessible Pinnacle on Skye and also Carn Cloich-mhuillinn in the Cairngorms. He was keeping the latter as his final mountain, hoping to do it from an SMC meet at his home at Lindertis.

CHAPTER 3

The Reverend A. E. Robertson, the First Munroist

In September 1901, A. E. Robertson climbed Meall Dearg on the Aonach Eagach along with his wife and Lord Moncrieff. History had been made for Meall Dearg was his final Munro and he kissed the cairn first, and then his wife.

Robertson was a gentleman climber and a fine mountaineer. He was equally expert on snow and rock and he climbed in the Alps as well as in his beloved Scotland. Born in 1870, he quickly developed a love of the hills and he climbed Goat Fell on Arran alone at the age of twelve.

He enjoyed his position in society and he demanded the best in everything. When he bought his equipment he obtained his ice-axe from Simond, his aneroid from Lord Kelvin, his compass from Whites and his boots from James Wright of Edinburgh. He was a talented craftsman and made the table for the Charles Inglis-Clarke Memorial Hut under Ben Nevis. For his photos he would carry a whole plate camera up Carn Mor Dearg or to Coire Mhic Fhearchair. He delved into the history of the Highlands and he published a pamphlet *Old Tracks and Cross Country Routes of the North West Highlands*. He was Chairman of the Rights-of-Way Society, and President of the SMC from 1930–32.

Like Munro, he used the shelter provided by the keepers' and stalkers' cottages, but he was more discerning. After Ladhar Bheinn he had intended to spend the night at Skiary but was so put off by the dirty rooms and lack of beer or whisky, that he went on to Kinlochhourn. However, he records pleasant hospitality with keepers at Steall, Glen Dessarry, Carnoch and Kinlochquoich. He writes: 'Make me of the shepherds' houses, for the people in the glen are not spoilt by the vulgar products of modern civilisation and are kind, courteous and hospitable. In all my wanderings I have never been refused a night's shelter in a keeper's house or shepherd's shieling'.

Robertson enjoyed his comforts and had a more leisurely approach to the hills than Munro. He writes: 'We found Ben Doran an awful grind but we lay on the snow for an hour on the summit, basking and smoking our pipes and revelling in the view. The descent provided us with a 2,000ft glissade'. He also enjoyed long holidays. Three months at McDonald's at Coylumbridge in 1894. A ten-day walking tour at Easter 1895 in Morar, Knoydart and Kintail. Three months holiday in 1898 which gave him 75 Munros, and another three months in 1899 when he did a further 72.

On one expedition Robertson hired a trap to Loch Ericht Lodge. Beside the Culra Burn, he met a party of men supposed to be mending the path, but all fast asleep. 'I gave a shout and how they jumped, they thought I was Sir John Ramsden the Laird'. He ascended Ben Alder and was put up at McCook's at Benalder Lodge. The next day he went over Geal Charn, Aonach Beag and Beinn Eibhinn, had tea at the keeper's house at Lublea and continued to Moy Inn for the night.

Robertson used a bicycle for the inaccessible mountains and he was able to cycle up Glen Strathfarrar as far as Monar Lodge, Glen Cannich to the west end of Loch Mullardoch and to the west of Loch Quoich.

On the completion of his Munros, he recommended to the SMC that for rock-work the Cuillins, Nevis, Glencoe, Torridon and the Teallachs were best and for snow-work Mam Soul, Sgurr nan Conbhairean, the Cairngorms, Ben Alder and Beinn Heasgarnich. He wrote: 'I look back upon the days spent pursuing this quest as among the best spent days of my life'.

Robertson died in 1958 at the age of 88, and the SMC erected a memorial bridge to him over the river Elchaig to facilitate access to the Falls of Glomach.

Good route planning can make the ascent of the Munros a relatively simple business. J. Dow completed all the Munros after the age of 45. He wrote at the end in 1933: 'Never once did I fail to return to a hot bath and a comfortable bed and very rarely did I miss dinner. The return was always to a fully equipped and licensed hotel.'

CHAPTER 4

My Final Munro

BIDEAN NAM BIAN 3,766ft/1150m

On the summit of Bidean nam Bian on 12 June 1971 a small party was gathered round the cairn; champagne corks were popping and toasts were being drunk. It was not the successful end to another epic climb for television but a party to celebrate the completion of the Scottish Munros.

Bidean nam Bian towers above the Glencoe peaks and with its many ridges and rock faces it is undoubtedly one of the finest mountains in Scotland. For this reason I carefully kept it virgin for my final Munro. Other reasons for this selection were that it is fairly easily accessible to the south and it is very near the traditional Kingshouse Hotel for a mammoth party after the ascent.

Fifteen friends and relations made up the assault party while an equal number remained in the Glen. We left the Meeting of Three Waters for the Lost Valley on a warm and dry but overcast day. My brother, Oliver Gilbert, remarked that it was just as well it was my final Munro since it was taking a large support party, carrying unheard of goodies to get me to the summit. Hot soup, cold chicken and champagne were luxuries unheard of on any other Munro climbing expedition.

We were lucky with the weather for this, the Great

31

Day, when you consider what we might have experienced. For in mid-May 1898 there was 14ft of snow on the Ben Nevis plateau and in March 1950, 59 inches of rain were recorded at Kinlochquoich, including 8 inches on one day.

I was delighted that my father made the ascent with me. He accompanied me on my first and last Munro but missed 274 in between.

We had an hour by the cairn and my feelings were mixed. I was thrilled that a ten-year-dream had come true, for on many occasions I had longed for this moment, yet there was a feeling of deflation and loss when I realised that it was all over. Now I have adjusted to the new situation and I still return to Scotland at every opportunity and enjoy the mountains just as much. The adrenalin doesn't pump through my veins in the same way when I approach a summit and I enjoy what the mountains have to offer more from an aesthetic than a physical point of view.

We descended slowly and happily down the stony ridge to the col under Stob Coire nan Lochan then back to the Lost Valley and Kingshouse.

What a civilised day it was. Afternoon tea followed by a bath, and then dinner of roast venison, speeches, toasts, cigars and port. Sir Hugh Munro and the Reverend A.E. Robertson would have approved.

Much of the conversation was about the past for the Munros leave you rich in experience and romance which you can seldom share with others. Mention A'Mhaighdean, Lapaich or Ben Alder to a Munroist and see his eyes light up with a far away gleam. You are talking to a fellow traveller whose spirit is in the remote tops of the Highlands.

CHAPTER 5

The Far North

BEN KLIBRECK 3,154ft/961m
BEN HOPE 3,040ft/927m

25 June 1967   I climbed these two Munros of the far north, by myself, driving from Stoer where we were having a family holiday.

For Ben Klibreck I left the car on the A836 three miles from Altnaharra. It proved to be a most featureless and unattractive mountain, in shape rather like Skiddaw in the Lake District. I ascended up relentless grassy slopes in mist and drizzle to the summit cairn and returned the same way. 2 hours 40 minutes round trip.

I drove on to Ben Hope and parked just beyond the Broch at Dun Dornaigil. This time the round trip took only 2 hours 20 minutes. Ben Hope is altogether a more impressive mountain than Ben Klibreck and the west face is rocky and precipitous. Unfortunately I had driving rain for most of the time but I had odd glimpses of the view that must be excellent on better days.

CONIVAL 3,234ft/987m
BEN MORE ASSYNT 3,273ft/998m

8 September 1962   Trisha and I left Inchnadamph on a perfect day and walked up the path beside the Traligill

Burn. This is a limestone area and the water of the burn disappears into an underground cave. Other caves and passages abound in this area. We did not stop to explore but continued up on to the main shoulder just north of Conival. The higher slopes of Conival are of quartzite rocks and are clean and smooth.

The ridge continues over Conival to Ben More Assynt and it overlooks wild rugged country with the grey glaciated Lewisian gneiss holding many lochans in its pockets and depressions. Quinag to the north-west stood out prominently from the other mountains.

We retraced our footsteps to Conival and then dropped down to Glen Dubh for our walk back to Inchnadamph for tea. A 5 hour round trip. In Glen Dubh we found a few clumps of white heather which was very fitting as we were on our honeymoon.

CHAPTER 6

Beinn Dearg Forest

EIDIDH NAN CLACH GEALA 3039ft/928m
MEALL NAN CEAPRAICHEAN 3192ft/977m
BEINN DEARG 3547ft/1084m
CONA' MHEALL 3200ft/980m
AM FAOCHAGACH 3120ft/954m

7 September 1962 From Glensguaib in Inverlael
Forest my wife and I walked over Eididh nan Clach
Geala and Meall nan Ceapraichean. It was pouring
with rain and this turned to sleet high up; there was
even fresh snow on Meall nan Ceapraichean. We were
on compass bearings for most of the day and we only
caught fleeting glimpses of the attractive lochan under
the semi circle of cliffs under Eididh nan Clach Geala.
Glen na Sguaib is a good way in to these mountains
which provide pleasant and easy walks.

10 September 1962 Three days later in much better
weather we ventured into the Beinn Dearg group.
Leaving the car on the A835 near Loch Droma we
walked across into Glen Mhucarnaich and gained
access to the broad southern shoulder of Beinn Dearg.
This was a poor route as Glen Mhucarnaich was very
badly peat hagged. On many occasions we had to jump
five feet or so down into black ooze and fight our way
out up the slippery slopes on the other side.

Once on the slopes of Beinn Dearg the going was
easy and we passed patches of old snow that had

survived the summer. The views were good, down Loch
Broom to the Summer Isles, the Fannichs and naturally
to An Teallach which looks impressive from any angle.

We walked round the north-east shoulder to Cona'
Mheall and then descended quite steeply down a fine
rocky ridge to Loch Coire Lair. Continuing eastwards
up tedious boulder strewn slopes we gained the top of
Am Faochagach, surely one of the most featureless and
boring of the Munros. Even when we had descended
towards Loch Coire Lair we had two miles of dreadful
bog and peat hag to cross before we regained the road.

In early June 1973 I was in Ullapool on a gorgeous
spring morning and I was drawn to the Beinn Dearg
range again. There had been fresh snow over 3,000ft
during the night yet the morning was warm and sunny. I
drove along the Inverlael forestry track to Glensguaib
and struck over the hills due east to reach the back of
Eididh nan Clach Geala. On this occasion I could fully
appreciate the remote lochan and corrie on the
southern side. A golden eagle soared overhead. I
walked round on to Meall nan Ceapraichean and up to
the shoulder under Beinn Dearg. From here I detoured
a mile to take in the summit of Cona' Mheall where I
had lunch. I retraced my steps and then climbed steeply
beside a huge snow field, still corniced, to the summit
of Beinn Dearg. In just under four hours I had climbed
four Munros; I was feeling fit and I thoroughly enjoyed
every step. Unfortunately the weather had been
deteriorating all morning and now it was snowing hard.
I followed the broad north-west ridge down to Glen na
Sguaib and reached the car in pouring rain.

Three years later, in April, I repeated this superb
round of four Munros with my eleven-year-old son
Tim. A hot and sunny day had brought out thousands

of tiny frogs which teemed in the burns and lochans. As in 1976, a golden eagle appeared on Eididh nan Clach Geala and ptarmigan and snow bunting on Beinn Dearg. A 7-hour round from Inverlael.

In the following year, 1977, spring came exceptionally late to the Highlands and in mid-April there was general snow cover down to 1700ft. Even little Ben Ghobhlach at the mouth of Loch Broom wore a white cap.

Tim and I set off for Am Faochagach from the road bridge at the west end of Loch Glascarnoch. At regular intervals dreadful squalls came driving across the hills bringing hail, spindrift and gale force winds. To reach our objective it was necessary to wade two big burns, there was no alternative, and the freezing water came up to my knees and to Tim's waist.

On the mountain itself we toiled up slopes of deep soft snow. High up on the summit ridge a frightful squall hit us and I had to hold Tim to stop him being blown away. We battled on with faces iced up and trousers frozen solid. It was almost impossible to look ahead but, just when I decided we must retreat, the summit cairn appeared through the mist.

A hasty return left us numb and shattered. What a fight to gain what is after all a fairly low and insignificant Munro!

SEANA BHRAIGH 3,041ft/927m

This is a remote Munro but it can be made more accessible by driving six miles along Glen Achall to near Rhidorroch Old Lodge. I have climbed Seana Bhraigh three times and each time I have done the drive. Once without permission when I found the estate gates open and I hid the car under some trees, once when my wife dropped Tim and myself at the lodge and then she returned to Ullapool, and again with permission from the estate.

28 July 1967 The first occasion was on a muggy summer's day with persistent drizzle, although in spite of this Glen Achall looked very beautiful with a large burn running into the loch and imposing cliffs on the north side.

I crossed the burn under a deep gorge and struck up Glen Douchary. I passed some magnificent cascades and waterfalls, one in particular was outstanding. The river Douchary with a good deal of water running fell a hundred feet sheer into a vast amphitheatre and at the bottom of this stood a huge pointed boulder on which grew a Caledonian pine. The amphitheatre had good flat grassy areas which I marked for a future campsite.

I bypassed Meall nam Bradhan and climbed Seana Bhraigh by the north-west shoulder. The big northern corrie of Seana Bhraigh falls right away from the summit cairn to the lochan 1,500ft below and to the north Strath Mulzie can be traced back for miles. To the south, upper Glen a' Chadha Dheirg had some imposing looking cliffs of bare rock.

It was warm enough for a quick dip in the Douchary river as I returned in the afternoon.

In September 1973, with Oliver Gilbert, I returned to Seana Bhraigh by the Glen Douchary route, and the amphitheatre and waterfall had lost none of their romantic appeal. It took us 3¼ hours from Rhidorroch Old Lodge to the summit of Seana Bhraigh. Unfortunately when we opened the rucksack on a small ledge just over the lip of the cliffs we found that lunch had been left in the car. Oliver, a professional botanist and ecologist, spent some time examining some most interesting plants and lichens on the cliffs before hunger and a cold wind drove us back.

We returned through the impressive ravine carrying the Allt nan Caorach near Lochan Badan Glasliath. It is a deep and narrow ravine, a mile long, with steep sides. Certainly a lonely and fascinating place. Back to the car after a 5½ hour round trip.

In April 1978 Tim and I were dropped at Rhidorroch Old Lodge and we walked past the spectacular falls of the Douchary river up into Glen Douchary. We climbed Meall nam Bradhan and continued round to Seana Bhraigh. The north-east corrie was ringed with cornices but most of the snow had disappeared and hundreds of deer were grazing on the mossy plateau.

Back down in Upper Glen Douchary we saw a golden eagle and thought that the fine cliffs at the mouth of Creige Duibhe must contain an eyrie, but we looked in vain.

Instead of returning down to Glen Achall we forced our way across rough and trackless country to meet the path in Strath Nimhe and eventually made rendezvous at Leckmelm beside Loch Broom. 6½ hours.

CHAPTER 7

Ben Wyvis

BEN WYVIS 3429ft/1046m

6 April 1967   This vast mountain, which carries a good snow cover late into the year, dominates the view north across the Beauly Firth as one is driving down the A9 into Inverness. It has few distinct features and is tiresome to ascend mainly because the south and west flanks are heavily afforested, with the trees still young, and none of the forest rides or fire breaks seem to go in the right direction. Alan Wedgwood confessed to me that Ben Wyvis was the only Munro that he set out to climb but gave up through sheer boredom.

The first time I ascended Ben Wyvis I left the car at Garbat, five miles north of Garve on the A835. It was cloudy and snowing but on compass bearing you cannot really go wrong if you continue ever on upwards until the summit ridge is reached. The western slopes of the mountain can be ascended anywhere. I reached the ridge fifty yards from the summit trig point and found a very wintry scene: new snow and patches of bare ice where the ridge had been blown clear. I did not linger long in the icy wind but ran down again to the car. A 3 hour round trip.

In March 1974 I was driving along the A835 on such a lovely morning that I could not resist another ascent of Ben Wyvis. Again from Garbat I negotiated the frightful afforested area and found it even worse than before with the trees now larger.

I found the endless slopes below the summit very hot and tiring but reached the summit in hazy sunshine after 2½ hours. There was general snow cover over 3,000ft. If I go up this mountain again it will be from the east side!

Time is a great healer and, in spite of my 1974 comments, Tim and I were drawn to Ben Wyvis on a perfect early November's day in 1978.

From Garbat we selected a forest ride which took us to the bealach on the north-west side of the mountain, between Carn Gorm and Tom a'Choinnich. This allowed us to traverse the summit ridge to An Cabar. On the main summit, Glas Leathad Mor (3429ft), a little early snow had drifted against the cairn, but the bonus was a stupendous view stretching from Foinaven to Torridon and Mam Soul, and from the Cromarty Firth to the Cairngorms.

A pleasant descent of the west ridge of An Cabar took us back to Garbat after a 3½ hour round trip, and we followed this by tea at the Aultguish Hotel.

My faith in Ben Wyvis is restored and I am horrified by the plans, being mooted at the time of writing, to build a funicular railway up the mountain from Strathpeffer.

CHAPTER 8

Fisherfield Forest

AN TEALLACH 3483ft/1062m
SLIOCH 3217ft/980m
MULLACH COIRE MHIC FHEARCHAIR 3327ft/1019m
SGURR BAN 3194ft/989m
A'MHAIGHDEAN 3060ft/960m
BEINN TARSUINN 3080ft/930m

My formative years were spent inseparable from W. H. Murray's *Undiscovered Scotland* which contains a vivid account of An Teallach:

> I turned to look up at An Teallach. The first of the moonlight was filtering between the pinnacles. The vast circle of their frozen walls stared down at a frozen loch – a sombre circle, but lifting high in the centre to that five-pointed crown rimmed by light.

30 March 1960   Thus my expectancy was high when Alan Wedgwood, Robin Richards and I drove down from the Destitution Road to Little Loch Broom.

I need not have worried for we were spellbound by the sudden view of the stupendous corries, ringed by black teeth, towering above us. The fact that we had spent the previous three days on Liathach, Beinn Eighe and Beinn Alligin in no way blunted our appreciation of An Teallach, perhaps the greatest of all the giants of the North West.

The exceptional weather continued and our traverse of the ridge, from Sail Liath, over Sgurr Fiona to

Bidein a'Ghlas Thuill was made in summer weather.

I often look back to those four magnificent late March days. They certainly sparked off my love of the hills of the north and they helped to direct my mountaineering interests away from rock-climbing and more towards hill-walking.

19 August 1964 I first climbed Slioch alone on a wet summer's day from Kinlochewe. I walked alongside Loch Maree into Glen Bianasdail but I did not realise the river was bridged lower down and I had considerable difficulty in crossing it. I ascended into the wide corrie on the east side and gained the south ridge which leads to the summit. There was a snow shower on the summit plateau. Back the same way in worsening weather. 4½ hours.

In March 1975 I went up Slioch with a party of boys. There had been several days of heavy snow and the day was overcast with squalls of snow and sleet. In Glen Bianasdail we saw a herd of five wild goats. They were mottled white and grey, they were very shaggy and had magnificent horns. In the upper corrie the snow was between knee and waist deep and we floundered about, stumbling over buried rocks and falling into hidden streams. We made for the south-west ridge hoping for less snow but this entailed a difficult steep ascent on unstable snow over frozen grass. The little loch on the shoulder was frozen and bleak and the wind and snow whistled past us. The final steep slopes on to Slioch's summit took us a long time, fighting through waist deep snow. We took it in turns to take the lead wading 100 steps before changing the leader. The ascent took 5½ hours from Kinlochewe.

21 July 1965 My brother Christopher and I set off from Kinlochewe for A'Mhaighdean which had the

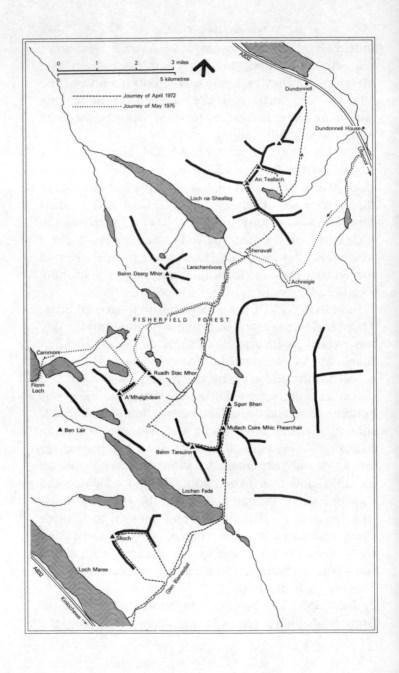

reputation of being one of the remotest, if not the remotest, Munro. It was overcast and drizzling as we passed the small group of cottages which make up the Heights of Kinlochewe and turned off up Glen na Muice. At the east end of Lochan Fada we climbed the hillside towards Mullach Coire Mhic Fhearchair, but once on the ridge had to lose 500ft before the final ascent to the quartzite-capped summit. We were hot and bathed in perspiration under our coat of Flypel, liberally applied to ward off the swarms of clegs.

An hour later we reached Sgurr Ban and decided we had enough time and energy to press on to A'Mhaighdean. We quickly lost 2,000ft, descending to the other Glen na Muice south of Strathnasheallag. Five miles down the glen we could just make out the green fields surrounding the remote bothy Shenavall under An Teallach. To the north was the black serrated ridge of Beinn Dearg Mhor. It was rough going to reach the base of A' Mhaighdean but once on the lower slopes we climbed rapidly into the mist again. At 5.15 p.m. we reached the small summit cairn perched on the edge of some impressive cliffs overlooking the dark waters of the Dubh Loch and Gorm Loch Mor.

We descended on a compass bearing which brought us near to the north-west end of Lochan Fada and we had 2 hours of terrible going alongside the loch until our former track was gained once more. We reached Kinlochewe at 9.45 p.m. after a nearly 12-hour day. Our total halts were not more than 20 minutes altogether and it was one of the longest days I have had on the hills.

In April 1972 together with Paul Hawksworth and a party from Ampleforth College Mountaineering Club I walked over from Kinlochewe to Dundonnell. We took tents and provisions for four days and managed to climb most of the Munros in the Strathnasheallag, Fisherfield and Letterewe Forest areas.

We walked up into Glen Bianasdail and left our rucksacks while we made an unencumbered ascent of Slioch. We had a long rest in the sunshine on the summit enjoying panoramic views. This was one of the very few occasions that I have enjoyed a spell relaxing on the summit of a Munro. It is usually far too cold, too misty and the schedule is too tight to allow such luxury. We finally tore ourselves away and continued round the ridge to Sgurr an Tuill Bhain before dropping down the glen to retrieve our packs. It was hot work ascending upper Glen Bianasdail and then fording the burn to Lochan Fada-side.

We found the most perfect and idyllic camp site imaginable in a sheltered bay at the east end of Lochan Fada. Soft cropped grass, a shingle beach and panoramic views. There was a glorious red sunset reflected in the loch and ringed by Slioch, Ben Lair, Beinn Tarsuinn and A'Mhaighdean. Later we lit a driftwood fire as the clear night produced a hard frost. *20 April 1972* The following morning we had a perfect dawn and we saw a flock of geese in V formation flying over Beinn Tarsuinn. We left our rucksacks on the col below Mullach Coire Mhic Fhearchair and then ascended the peak and continued to Sgurr Ban. The north facing slopes still held big snow fields but the ridges were free. From the Sgurr Ban col we traversed the western slopes of the Mullach to regain our packs.

On to Beinn Tarsuinn next where I had a flask of whisky to celebrate my final separate 3,000ft mountain on the mainland of Britain. The mountain was resurveyed and added to Munro's Tables well after they were first published. It was a worthy Munro, having an interesting ridge and steep north-facing cliffs. The wind had swung round to the west and clouds were gathering over An Teallach. We camped early on the col under A'Mhaighdean.

We awoke to drizzle and low cloud so we beat down Glen na Muice, crossed the river by the Larachantivore suspension bridge, forded the Abhain Strath na Sealga and reached Shenavall bothy after 2½ hours. Glen na Muice was dark and lowering and we were impressed by the huge crag to the south of Glen na Muice Beag known as Junction Buttress.

Shenavall is a really comfortable and solid bothy with wooden floors and rooms upstairs. We collected wood from the riverside and lit a huge fire. Later in the evening the clouds lifted above Beinn Dearg Mhor which looked as rugged as ever. It is a perfect mountain with a high horseshoe corrie, then ringed with snow and the gullies picked out as white streaks.

The next morning we were off early up nearly 3,000ft of mountainside to Sail Liath on An Teallach. On the main ridge the rocks were glazed with ice and frost feathers had formed in the keen east wind. As the clouds rose and the day improved we had a memorable traverse of all the pinnacles and tops to Bidein a' Ghlas Thuill, the principal summit of An Teallach. The view ranged from Nevis to Mam Soul, Foinaven, Suilven, Skye and the Outer Isles. The northern gullies were full of snow and the cliffs hung with icicles, but the rock was dry and we had a most enjoyable scramble over the pinnacles of rough Torridonian sandstone and over Lord Berkeley's Seat. It was a day in a thousand.

From the white quartzite east top of Bidein a' Ghlas Thuill we descended the slope of jumbled blocks of rock to Loch Toll an Lochain. We had a long rest in the sun at the centre of the amphitheatre and several boys swam.

The Gods owed us this perfect day as on my previous visit to Shenavall in late October 1970 I had dreadful storms and rain. Mike and Jackie Hodson and I left the A832 road-bridge four miles south of Dundonnell at 4.30 p.m. carrying tents and food for four days camping at Loch Toll an Lochain. We were carrying too much weight and walking too slowly and it was rapidly becoming dark and the rain was increasing in intensity. After the Dundonnell–Achnegie track is passed the ground is very broken and we came on a line of cliffs nearly 200ft high which we had to descend. These cliffs were not marked on the one inch map. I became separated from the others in the darkness so proceeded alone to Loch Toll an Lochain. A full gale was now blowing and it took me over an hour, torch in mouth, to put up my Blacks Mountain tent and flysheet. Only stones on the pegs and on the snow-flap kept it down in the gale. I had a disturbed night as the wind came in great buffets roaring up the corrie and shaking the tent which strained and heaved but held firm.

In the morning, at 10.15 a.m., the Hodsons arrived in the pouring rain. They had been camping a mile down the hillside and were soaked to the skin and nearly all in. The metal tent pole of their Jamet tent had snapped in the night and from 3 a.m. onwards Mike had held up the broken end. Of course the rain came in and by morning three inches of water was slopping about inside. They had breakfast with me and then we packed up and traversed the Sail Liath shoulder to reach Shenavall. In the conditions and with a heavy pack I got into difficulties descending some minor crags and had to retrace my steps several hundred feet to find an easier way.

However all was forgotten at Shenavall. We wrung out the Hodson's sleeping bags, lit a fire and started on the whisky. It was heaven. Later Paul and Peter Hawksworth arrived from Dundonnell. We dried them out and they joined the festivities.

The rain continued throughout the night and next morning we needed to go out for wood. We found bog-wood and logs beside the swollen river and carried back a rotting wooden boat from Larachantivore Cottage. This was the far side of Strathnasheallag and entailed wading two rivers.

After lunch, feeling frustrated, we crossed the rivers again and climbed Beinn Dearg Mhor. The gale was trying to pluck us off the narrow ridge and we had no view.

That night was All Hallows-een but the witches stayed at home. It was as wild a night as I have experienced, comparable to 14 January 1968. Thank God we were not camping at Loch Toll an Lochain. We later learned it was the worst gale for three years. Shenavall shook on its stone foundations and the morning found Strathnasheallag a lake and the rivers quite unfordable. We returned to the Dundonnell Hotel for comfort and an excellent dinner.

Contrast again in mid-April 1981 on an An Teallach traverse from Corrie Hallie to Dundonnell with my family which included William (9) and Lucy (11). It was an extremely hot and airless day with only a few patches of snow remaining high up in the gullies. An extensive heather fire was raging on Sail Liath and we had an extraordinary time finding a safe way through the smoke and flames. Fire is a mountain hazard very rarely met with on the hills of Britain.

In the strong spring sunshine the sandstone on Corrag Bhuidhe buttress was warm to the touch and our throats were parched. A leisurely descent from Bidein a' Ghlas Thuill by the tourist route to Dundonnell and an evening walk back along the road to the car, enjoying the early daffodils in the beautiful gardens of Dundonnell House. 9¼ hours.

BEINN A' CHLAIDHEIMH 3000ft/914m

1 June 1974 Beinn a' Chlaidheimh is a mountain only recently promoted to Munro status following a resurvey. It is a remote mountain south of Strathnasheallag and it is on the north end of the ridge beyond Sgurr Ban.

I set out at midnight from the track-end one mile south of Dundonnell House. It was overcast and raining on and off but it was never really dark and I could easily follow the track to Achneigie. It was two hours walk to Achneigie with the night silent and eerie except for the wind and the occasional sheep or lamb. I forded the river and struck up towards my objective which I could see outlined against the sky. The terrain was boggy and there were outcrops of Torridonian sandstone which I scrambled through; I heard a fox bark quite close by.

The final ridge was narrow and exciting and the actual summit was on the southernmost end. I reached the cairn at 3.45 a.m. and although it was not cold I did not linger. It was by now quite light and I nearly walked into a nest of young dunlin with the mother performing a broken wing act nearby. I also passed near a herd of young stags with their antlers in velvet.

I reached the car at 6.45 a.m. in excellent spirits and later had breakfast at the Dundonnell Hotel.

RUADH STAC MHOR 3014ft/918m

31 May 1975 Ruadh Stac Mhor is the third new Munro to be elevated to the official list following a resurvey. It also happens to be one of the remotest mountains in Scotland, lying in the heart of the Fisherfield Forest, and I found it hard to decide whether to attack it from Dundonnell, Kinlochewe or Poolewe. In the end I decided to include it along with A'Mhaighdean in a night walk from Dundonnell to Poolewe.

It was a clear cold evening as I set out at 10 p.m. along the Achneigie track from Dundonnell House. For the first mile the track passes through mixed woodland of pine, birch and alder and the leaves just out were a delicate shade of green. The gorse and broom were in full flower and there were bluebells under the trees, a cuckoo was singing. The gullies and folds of An Teallach were picked out in relief by the last rays of the sun and I did not worry too much about the bank of grey cloud building up in the north.

I spent a few minutes memorising the map and some important bearings because I had not brought a torch and knew from a similar night's walk, the previous year, that it did not become light enough to see the map until 3.30 a.m. The first star appeared at 11 p.m. but it never became completely dark.

As soon as I reached the Strathnasheallag path I caught a whiff of wood smoke and realised that Shenavall bothy, although still a mile away, must be in use. I found there a man and a boy sitting in front of a good fire and I joined them for a few minutes and ate some sandwiches.

The Sheallag river was very low and I was able to cross it dry-shod but the next half mile across the wet bog to Larachantivore was hideous as I could not see well enough to pick out the dry parts. Grey patches of ground would look like stone only to be liquid mud and leave me cursing with a boot full of ooze. I was disappointed to find the suspension bridge above Larachantivore Cottage damaged and almost useless. The centre planks were missing and the cables were not held together leaving me performing the splits over mid-stream. With a heavy pack and the river in flood the crossing would have been highly unpleasant.

For the next two miles I missed the path and blundered my way through the heather and rocks up into Glen na Muice Beag before I found it again. It was now overcast and snowing but it was a great relief to be on the Carnmore path which was well constructed and easy to follow even in the bad light.

At 2.30 a.m. I reached the small loch named Lochan Feith Mhic'illean at the watershed, this was one of my reference points and I turned off on a bearing up the slopes of Ruadh Stac Mhor. From the map this mountain looks to be easy angled and uninteresting. However, it is a fine sharp rocky peak and is ringed with broken cliffs. The snow was something of a problem for it was settling above 1,500ft and was two inches deep already. It was difficult negotiating the rocks and boulders for they were horribly slippery and I could imagine the consequences of a broken leg. I had no ice-axe or gloves and my face and clothes were iced up and frozen. Although this mountain was a new final Munro for me I did not linger for a moment at the cairn. I was ill-equipped for such a mountain in what amounted to winter conditions.

At 4 a.m. I reached the col under A'Mhaighdean after a tedious and tricky descent down steep rocks from Ruadh Stac Mhor. Dawn had arrived but it was still snowing hard. I ate an early breakfast and felt much better.

A'Mhaighdean had sizeable areas of old snow on the north side and I kicked my way up to keep warm, and arrived at the small summit cairn above the south face at 5 a.m. I had intended to descend the sharp north-west ridge, but in the unexpectedly severe conditions I decided against it and went down to the east end of Fuar Loch Mor instead. I felt very unsure of myself without an axe and I took the steep snowy slopes very gingerly, whereas with an axe for security I would have romped down.

At 6.45 a.m. I reached the Dubh Loch and I could see the remote farm of Carnmore which is supplied by boat from across the Fionn Loch. The clouds were dispersing and I had some sunshine for the long, long walk out to Poolewe. The track was poor and non-existent in places, but it went under the most impressive north face of Ben Airidh Charr which has a large area of vertical or overhanging clean grey rock. At Loch Kernsary I was once again out of the bleak mountains and the loch looked beautiful in the early morning sunshine with luxuriant growth of gorse, broom, rowan and birch. There were cuckoos and curlews and waders feeding by the loch-side. This loch and the surrounding estate was given to the young Osgood MacKenzie, who built Inverewe Gardens, by his father so the boy could pursue his own sporting interests.

I finally reached Poolewe at 10.15 a.m. after a most enjoyable night's walk. Surely this is one of the finest mountain walks in Scotland. Looking back east to the snow covered Beinn Eighe and Ben Lair I realised that even after 279 Munros I still had not appreciated the possibility of winter conditions on the last day of May.

Two days later, on June 2, I drove south through two inches of snow on the Drumochter Pass in some of the worst June weather ever recorded.

CHAPTER 9

The Fannichs

MEALL A' CHRASGAIDH 3062ft/934m
SGURR MOR 3637ft/1110m
BEINN LIATH MHOR FANNAICH 3120ft/954m
SGURR NAN CLACH GEALA 3561ft/1093m
SGURR NAN EACH 3026ft/923m
A'CHAILLEACH (Fannichs) 3276ft/999m
SGURR BREAC 3420ft/1000m
MEALL GORM 3109ft/949m
AN COILEACHAN 3015ft/923m

12 September 1962 From a camp in upper Glen Mor,
a mile on the Dundonnell side of the Corrieshalloch
Gorge, on a warm and misty day, I climbed the long
northern shoulder of Meall a' Chrasgaidh and continued along the grassy ridge over Sgurr Mor and Beinn
Liath Mhor. Returning along the ridge I skirted Sgurr
Mor on the west side and reached the col under Sgurr
nan Clach Geala. This mountain has the best rock face
in the Fannich range; a triangular shaped cliff 800ft
high and split by deep fissures. I had time to continue
one mile south down the ridge from Sgurr nan Clach
Geala to take in Sgurr nan Each, a pointed eminence
on the ridge, just over 3,000ft high.

I returned to the road down the long glen to the west
of Sgurr nan Clach Geala and Meall a' Chrasgaidh
whose name is not marked on the one inch map. Back
in camp after 6 hours.

2 November 1970 After three appallingly wet and

stormy days at Shenavall, described elsewhere, my friends left for the south but I stayed on for an extra day hoping for better things. As it turned out I didn't get them!

On a cold, wet and windy morning I left the car on the A832 at the nearest point to Loch a' Bhraoin and traversed A'Chailleach and Sgurr Breac. I walked up the broad north ridge of Sgurr Breac before traversing west below the summit to reach the col under A'Chailleach. After climbing this mountain I returned eastwards to Sgurr Breac.

The conditions were among the foulest I have met. I was soon soaked to the skin by the gales of rain and at the 2,900ft level there was 'silver rain'. The ground was covered in ice where the rain fell and immediately froze. My clothes likewise turned to armour. The cold numbed me from the waist down and I couldn't face the wind. After Sgurr Breac I gave up all hope of continuing to Meall Gorm and returned down the eastern slopes to the glen. At the bottom of the glen I had a nasty crossing of the burn in flood, it was waist deep, to reach the bridge at the east end of Loch a' Bhraoin.

31 March 1971 On a grey and drizzly day, Paul Hawksworth and I left our friends festering in the Ling Hut in Glen Torridon and drove round to Loch Glascarnoch north of the Fannichs. From the road we had 2 hours of hard slog up to Loch Li under Meall Gorm. The Li glen was open, heathered, hagged, morained, wet and quite pathless. It was muggy with wet cloud and no view whatsoever.

There were large snow patches on Meall Gorm and near the summit we found a rough stone-built shelter, today full of snow. Stupidly we had left our ice-axes behind and it took us two attempts to find a way up a steep snow slope and through a small cornice to gain the ridge. By the cairn it was mild and absolutely still, rare conditions for mountain summits in March.

We continued by compass bearing to An Coileachan and then came down past Loch Gorm and several other lochans to Glen Li. Loch Gorm looked vast and grey as we could only see a short way across owing to the mist. It seemed a long way back to the car alongside the large and free-flowing Abhainn Torrain Duibh. A round trip of 6½ hours.

I was back in the range in August 1974 with my son, Timothy Gilbert (aged 10), when we had a leisurely day, leaving the road two miles east of Braemore Junction and climbing Beinn Liath Mhor, Sgurr Mor and Meall a' Chrasgaidh. Up the north ridge of Beinn Liath Mhor and then on over moss and flat stones to the big cairn on Sgurr Mor. It was a perfect sunny day with a tearing wind, although warm enough in the sheltered glens for us to swim. Apart from a mile long peat haggy stretch at the bottom of Meall a' Chrasgaidh the going was gentle and easy all the way. 6 hours.

I can thoroughly recommend this circuit which, although including three Munros, makes a leisurely day, suitable for all the family. In July 1982 we ambled round in warm sunshine, stopping for a brew on the summit of Beinn Liath Mhor, and to guzzle ripe bilberries and cloudberries and have a swim beside Loch a' Mhadaidh.

CHAPTER 10

Achnasheen

FIONN BHEINN 3060ft/933m
MORUISG 3033ft/928m

21 August 1964 A short day doing two rather featureless and unattractive Munros. If the mountains had been just below 3,000ft rather than just above they would hardly merit a mention.

Fionn Bheinn is a grassy though shapely mountain. I ascended it easily from Achnasheen. Up and down in 2¼ hours.

Moruisg from Loch Sgamhain in a high wind. Round trip in 2¾ hours. It was a good view point for the Glen Strathfarrar and Monar Forest ranges.

SGURR NAN CEANNAICHEAN 3004ft/915m

25 August 1978 On the day of ascent (which was before the latest tinkering about with the list) I recorded this as my 280th and new final Munro.

Tim and I left the car just beyond the south end of Loch Sgamhain on the Achnasheen to Lochcarron road. We sought the top of an incline because the car, an ancient Citroen DS Safari, had a broken starter motor and it was quite impossible for us to push it.

We climbed up the long and tedious slopes to the summit of Moruisg. It was hot and sweaty in the sunshine and still air, with only the odd frog jumping across our path or the occasional train passing far below to relieve the monotony. After 1½ hours we reached Moruisg's summit and had lunch while appraising the lovely views over Torridon, the Coulin Forest, Maoille Lunndaidh and the Strathfarrar Hills.

Since our main objective of the day was Sgurr nan Ceannaichean, two miles to the south-west, we descended to a broad saddle before climbing up to its flat summit. Apart from some minor rock outcrops near the top the new Munro is mainly grassy and contains no notable features. An easy descent of the north ridge brought us back to the car after a 3½ hour round trip.

CHAPTER 11

Torridon

LIATHACH 3456ft/1054m

27 March 1960 I first traversed Liathach with Alan Wedgwood and Robin Richards. The conditions were ideal with only streaks of snow in the northern corries and patches on the highest slopes of Mullach an Rathain and Spidean a' Choire Leith.

The main ridge of Liathach has a reputation for being a formidable excursion. However only on the Am Fasarinen pinnacles is it really sharp and these can be avoided by taking a lower path on the south side. Of course in full winter conditions it would be a major expedition.

In March 1971 I traversed Liathach with a party of schoolboys. We scrambled up the steep corrie just west of the eastern summit. The scree and snow slopes gave no difficulty. The day improved to give us warm sunshine and good views and the pinnacles provided amusement with some boys hand traversing and others proceeding a' cheval. A scree gully descends from the ridge west of Mullach an Rathain to Torridon village and running down it we made the 3358ft descent to sea level in 35 minutes.

BEINN EIGHE 3309ft/1010m

28 March 1960 The day after our traverse of Liathach, Alan, Robin and I walked into Coire Dubh and round into Coire Mhic Fhearchair. As we surmounted the lip of the corrie by the loch we were confronted by the three huge buttresses rising 1500ft above us. The lower rocks consist of Torridonian sandstone and on this plinth sits the upper section of quartzite.

This corrie competes with Coire an Lochan of An Teallach, Coire Ardair of Creag Meagaidh and Coire Leis of Ben Nevis for the grandest corrie in Scotland.

We climbed Original Route on the Eastern Buttress. The climbing was excellent as the rock was so sound and the positions and stances so exposed. Quartzite shatters along definite planes and there were ledges everywhere. The left-hand buttress is the least steep of the three and the route we chose was about 'difficult' standard.

We walked along the ridge to Ruadh-Stac-Mor, the main peak, and then returned to the long main ridge leading east. The ridge provides a magnificent walk of nearly four miles with some quite exposed sections, in fact I prefer it to the Liathach ridge. From the eastern end we ran down peaty slopes and over burnt heather roots to reach the Kinlochewe Hotel.

In March 1971 I walked round into Coire Mhic Fhearchair with a party of boys. We walked fast and reached the corrie-loch in less than 1½ hours from the road. Several boys swam in the loch to cool off. We climbed straight up the slopes to the summit of Ruadh-Stac-Mor and then completed the main traverse of the ridge to Kinlochewe. A perfect spring day with little snow and we saw a golden eagle and snow bunting. 7½ hours.

Four years later in March 1975, after exceptionally heavy snow, it took us four hours to reach Coire Mhic Fhearchair swimming up to our thighs in fresh powder snow. It was snowing and freezing and we had to give up all hope of climbing up to Ruadh-Stac-Mor.

BEINN ALLIGIN 3232ft/985m

29 March 1960   Beinn Alligin is one of my favourite mountains. It rises steeply north of Loch Torridon and is conspicuous, with its deep cleft splitting the cliffs below the summit and the pinnacles or horns making up a horseshoe to the east.

It makes an easy first day for a holiday in Torridon and it cannot really be combined with any other ascent. One is always conscious of the magnificent view westwards across Loch Torridon to the sea, southwards to Beinn Damh and eastwards to Liathach and Beinn Eighe.

I have ascended the moutain three times, on each occasion in March and on each occasion in very different conditions.

In 1960 we [Gilbert, Wedgwood and Richards] had almost summer conditions with little or no snow. We climbed up from the road near the bridge over the Coire Mhic Nobuil burn to the shoulder Meall an Laoigh, marked 2904 on the map. From there it is an easy walk to Tom na Gruagaich, the subsidiary summit, and round the ridge to Sgurr Mhor 2332ft.

In 1971 with a party of boys from Ampleforth College Mountaineering Club we set off in mist and rain. However by the time we reached the summit the clouds had parted, the sun was out and we had a delightful and memorable traverse of the Rathains or Horns. As we descended back into Coire Mhic Nobuil the rocks and our clothes were steaming, and the final wisps of cloud were leaving the northern pinnacles of Liathach across the glen.

In 1975, again with a party of schoolboys, we had full winter conditions. There was deep powder snow right down to the road and the scramble up the rocks of Meall an Laoigh and the steep descent north from Tom na Gruagaich were exciting. The snow was like icing-sugar and it kept sliding away under our feet, very little rock was exposed. The big cleft looked very forbidding through the mist with the rock ledges piled with snow and the overhangs festooned with icicles.

We returned down the easy slopes to the west, reaching the road again just above Inver Alligin. 5½ hours round trip.

BEINN LIATH MHOR 3034ft/925m
SGORR RUADH 3142ft/960m
MAOL CHEAN-DEARG 3060ft/933m

20 August 1964 From the bridge in Glen Torridon, where the river flowing down Coire Dubh crosses the road, I followed the excellent track up into the Coulin Forest range. The track goes through the maze of hummocky moraines on to higher ground with many lochans and areas of bare Lewisian gneiss. I walked up to the summit of Beinn Liath Mhor and then descended south, skirting cliffs and lochans before reaching the north-west ridge of Sgorr Ruadh. This mountain has a long line of impressive cliffs on the north side. After reaching the summit, I descended the north-west ridge to gain the Bealach na Lice under Maol Chean-dearg. I climbed this third Munro directly up a loose scree gully which turned out to be much steeper than I first thought. I didn't fancy this gully for the descent so I took to the steep eastern slopes before easy ground enabled me to traverse round to Bealach na Lice once more. Back to the road after a strenuous 8 hours.

1   On the summit ridge of An Teallach in March 1960. This magnificent traverse sparked off my love of the hills of the north and helped to direct my mountaineering interests towards hill-walking.

2 A view across the southern summits of An Teallach from Bidean a'Ghlas Thuill, the highest peak of the massif. The mountains of the Fisherfield Forest can be seen in the distance. *Photo: Phil Cooper*

4   Liathach, perhaps the greatest of the Torridon giants, c
summits. Sections of this traverse involve awkward s

alker a challenging four-mile ridge-walk taking in five separate
requiring a delicate sense of balance. *Photo: John Cleare*

5   Alan Wedgwood (on Toll Creagach) polishes off the whisky to celebrate the completion of our four-day expedition over the peaks of Glen Affric and Glen Cannich in March 1962.

6   Oliver Gilbert checks the map on the summit of Creag a Mhaim on the South Kintail Ridge in March 1967.

7   A view from Ladhar Bheinn across Loch Hourn to Ben Sgritheall.
Photo: A. D. S. MacPherson

8 9   Two views in Knoydart in March 1963. Ladhar Bheinn (above) and Loch Hourn from the ridge above Barrisdale Bay. Two days later these summer conditions were replaced by storms as we fought for survival along the side of Loch Quoich.

CHAPTER 12

Glen Strathfarrar

BIDEIN A' CHOIRE SHEASGAICH 3102ft/945m
LURG MHOR 3234ft/986m
SGURR CHOINNICH 3260ft/999m
SGURR A' CHAORACHAIN 3452ft/1053m
MAOILE LUNNDAIDH 3295ft/1007m
SGURR FHUAR-THUILL 3439ft/1049m
SGURR A' CHOIRE GHLAIS 3554ft/1083m
CARN NAN GOBHAR (Strathfarrar) 3242ft/992m
SGURR NA RUAIDHE 3254ft/993m

25 July 1965   Christopher and I set out on a two-day expedition to cross Scotland from west to east traversing the Glen Strathfarrar range of mountains. We left Strathcarron Station at 9.30 a.m. carrying sleeping bags and snack meals only. Our luxuries were a tin of grapefruit juice and another of mandarin oranges.

We followed a path which meandered over the hills crossing a high col to Loch an Laoigh under our first objective, Bidein a' Choire Sheasgaich. It was muggy and overcast and we had a few showers of rain; indeed it took us 5 hours from Strathcarron Station to the top of Sheasgaich, an hour behind schedule. We continued to Lurg Mhor and were surprised to see Loch Monar below, the damming of which had increased its length by three miles or so not shown on our map.

After dropping down the steep northern slopes, we fed and watered ourselves by the Amhainn an Stratha

Mhoir before attempting the 2,000ft ascent up Sgurr
Choinnich by its south ridge. It was a slog in the
warmth of the late afternoon but the summit was in
cloud which refreshed us. Less than a mile east is Sgurr
a' Chaorachain, and we made good speed up this and
were rewarded by good views down Loch Monar and
across to An Riabhachan and Sgurr na Lapaich. We
passed sizeable patches of snow in the north-facing
gullies and saw many herds of deer. At 8.30 p.m. we
were on the col at 2,000ft, west of Maoile Lunndaidh,
quenching our thirst before the final ascent of the day.
We climbed the strangely terraced west ridge of Maoile
Lunndaidh and found a large herd of deer feeding off a
deep carpet of moss on the summit plateau. We were
tempted to lay out our sleeping bags here for the night,
but we resisted the temptation and located the Creag
Toll a' Choin cairn which is the true summit.

We stumbled far enough down the south-east ridge
to find water and a flat resting place for the night. It was
10.30 p.m. and we had been going hard for 13 hours.
The mandarin oranges went down easily and
deliciously. The night was overcast and cold, but we
slept well and rose at 6.30 a.m.

26 July 1965 Next morning we felt in fine fettle and
we started with 4 hours of rough going to the base of
our final group of four Munros. We attempted to
maintain our height above Loch Monar and this
involved many ascents, descents and traverses as three
deep glens have to be crossed. Once among the
Munros, we put Sgurr Fhuar-thuill, Sgurr a' Choire
Ghlais, Carn nan Gobhar and Sgurr na Ruaidhe behind
us in another 4 hours. The clouds were down early on
and we had to use the compass constantly, but the main
ridge was easy to follow. The mountains were rather

characterless, easy slopes to the south and cliffs to the north, each corrie guarding its own lochan. Sgurr a' Choire Ghlais, however, had a fine pointed rocky summit.

We descended out of the clouds to Deanie Lodge in Glen Strathfarrar in warm sunshine. At 3.15 p.m., we reached the private road leading to Monar Dam and were exceptionally lucky to pick up a lift in a Hydroelectric Board Land Rover which took us to Struy Bridge.

Glen Strathfarrar was very beautiful with its large river and stands of Caledonian pine, but the overall effect was marred by the hydroelectric access roads bulldozed out of the hillside and by the pylons. After a hitch to Beauly, we took a bus to Dingwall and caught the 6.15 p.m. train back to Strathcarron. All in all, it was a very pleasant and successful walk; needless to say we saw not a soul in this remote and wild region.

CHAPTER 13

Glen Cannich and Glen Affric

CARN NAN GOBHAR (Glen Cannich) 3251ft/992m
SGURR NA LAPAICH 3773ft/1150m
AN RIABHACHAN 3696ft/1129m
AN SOCACH 3503ft/1069m
SGURR NAN CEATHREAMHNAN 3771ft/1151m
AN SOCACH (Glen Affric) 3017ft/420m
MAM SODHAIL (MAM SOUL) 3862ft/1180m
CARN EIGE 3877ft/1183m
TOM A' CHOINICH 3646ft/1111m
TOLL CREAGACH 3452ft/1054m

I first climbed the Munros of Glen Cannich and Glen Affric in a marvellous four-day expedition in March 1962 with Alan Wedgwood. Alan had been reading old SMC journals and considered that what was good enough for Douglas, Raeburn and Inglis-Clark, was good enough for him. Thus he was going through a traditional phase and insisted on wearing an old tweed jacket throughout the expedition. This account is from a log book written up each night.

17 March 1962   9.30 p.m. in duvet jacket and sleeping bag. It is a cold clear night with a haloed moon. Dying embers of the fire outside and Vat 69 and pipe smoke within. Life at its best.

We arrived at the dam at the head of Loch Mullardoch at 5 p.m. Walked with our rucksacks, containing tent and provisions for four days, for an hour and pitched camp 600ft above the loch at the snow-line. Two trees by the stream provided wood for a fire on which we cooked soup and corned beef. There is a view across the loch to Toll Creagach and above us a corniced ridge. I shall sleep tonight in two sweaters, two pairs of socks and breeches.

18 March 1962 A somewhat energetic and rugged day. Now, 8.45 p.m., in rather damp bag but cheered by a large meal, pipe and whisky. We are camping at 2,500ft, well above the snow-line in a hidden, hanging valley ref. 115331 (we think).

We packed up and were off today at 8.30 and soon reached our first Munro, Carn nan Gobhar. We continued to Sgurr na Lapaich up steep snow and ice slopes, cutting steps. Finally, we reached a heavily corniced ridge, rocky and narrow, which led us to the summit. For much of the way we followed fox tracks.

So far so good, but leaving on a compass bearing in mist and sleet we got lost and spent the next 2 hours fighting our way down 1,500ft of steep snow and ice slopes, with frozen grass appearing at intervals. At one point we had to use the rope to lower our rucksacks down a 15ft ice bulge. At last the mist cleared for a moment and we saw Loch Mor below. The col to the An Riabhachan ridge lay 500ft above us to the left. This we reached by a snow gully. Fatigue was telling on us and our packs seemed heavy but we reached the 3,696ft top of An Riabhachan at 3.15 p.m.

Conditions were arctic with a virtual white-out. We proceeded along the ridge by compass bearing but again went wrong and were lost for an hour. Missing the next col again by several hundred feet, we emerged below the clouds and saw a hanging valley containing a big burn and a herd of deer. Then we saw Loch

Mullardoch far below and we identified our position and camped. We were below the 3,503 point on the one inch map, An Socach. Across the loch we could see for a moment the lower slopes of Carn Eige, but then the clouds came down again and rain set in for the night.

19 March 1962   9 p.m. It is a brilliantly clear night with a full moon – almost as bright as day. It is very cold, our polythene bag of water froze within minutes of the sun going down and I shall sleep in two sweaters and a duvet. Twelve hours ago we woke to low clouds and a snowstorm and we were in no hurry to move. At 11 a.m. though there was a break in the clouds and we left for An Socach. For 1,000ft our route lay up a steep snow bowl up which we could kick steps. The clouds were dispersing and the sun came out. Above us, two golden eagles soared, intrigued by our presence.

We broke through a small cornice to reach the summit ridge where an icy wind met us. We did not linger on top but quickly descended the western slopes to reach the glen near Loch Mhoicean. The glen contained several large herds of deer.

An hour later we paused in brilliant sunshine at Iron Lodge where we saw washing hanging on the line. At Carnach a shepherd showed us the way over a rickety suspension bridge to a short cut to the Falls of Glomach. We left the lush green glen and walked up to Loch Mhurchaidh. In the evening sun we had excellent views of Ben Attow, which was carrying a lot of snow. We camped at an idyllic spot below the north-west ridge of Sgurr nan Ceathreamhnan.

Without our packs we sped down the glen to see the Falls of Glomach. They were well worth the extra effort. A deep black gorge with 450ft of descent in three steps and a big river of melt-water plunging down. By 7 p.m. we were back in camp with red wisps of cloud overhead promising a superb day to come.

20 March 1962   We are feeling tired and happy after a great day that has been fully up to expectations. We are camping on snow at 2,800ft just below the col between Tom a' Choinich and Toll Creagach. This just leaves the latter mountain between us and the car for tomorrow morning. At the moment the snow is driving up the corrie and buffeting the tent. We have just had two immense brews and are about to attack the whisky.

This morning we were up at 6.30 a.m. to find a frozen stream and frozen boots even by our heads inside the tent. We were much fitter today and made short work of Sgurr nan Ceathreamhnan. It is a massive yet beautiful mountain with many subsidiary ridges and corries all holding snow. The sun came out and we could see Nevis, the Cuillins and the Torridon Hills; we could also see Mam Sodhail, our next objective, in the distance.

Some 2 hours later we were over the next Munro, An Socach marked 3017ft on the map, and we paused under Mam Sodhail and broke the ice on a tarn for a drink. It was clouding over now, but we could see the Five Sisters of Kintail and the Cluanie Hills south beyond Glen Affric. Mam Sodhail and Carn Eige are huge bulky mountains with mainly rounded shoulders. We could kick steps up the main ridge and we kept going without a break through the afternoon.

Beyond Carn Eige we had some hair-raising scrambling over a sharp ridge before walking over miles of wind swept wastes and tantalising hummocks. At last we saw Tom a' Choinich rising into the clouds, and we were lucky on the summit for the clouds parted and we could see plush green Glen Affric on one side and the

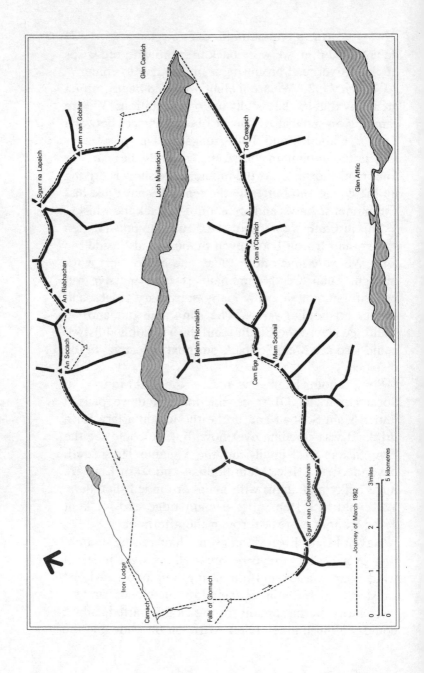

great waters of Loch Mullardoch on the other.

Running down 500ft of snow, we found a suitable camp site as the wind got up and it started snowing.

21 March 1962   We rose at 6.45 a.m. to find it snowing and several inches of new snow on the ground. After a hurried breakfast, we shook the snow from the tent, packed it up and quickly set off up the ridge for our last Munro–Toll Creagach. An hour later we were on the summit in the sun with the clouds getting thinner every moment. Soon we could see Sgurr na Lapaich across the loch and Tom a' Choinich looking huge and white three miles to the west.

Our spirits were sky high and we ran down 1,000ft of steep snow towards the head of Loch Mullardoch. We lay in the heather below the snow-line basking in the sunshine and finished off the whisky. Somewhat hazy memories remain, but we reached the dam and the car at 11.15 a.m. and later had a bath and lunch at the Drumnadrochit Hotel. That evening we joined the OUMC meet on Lochnagar.

In March 1967, I traversed Tom a' Choinich with a party of schoolboys. We went up Glen nam Fiadh and crossed west to east. The descent immediately below the cairn down the east ridge gave us some trouble. A beautiful sunny day, 6 hours from Affric Lodge. We were staying in a cottage near the Lodge. The estate workers were repairing flood damage from the previous December when Affric Lodge recorded 24 inches of rain. We saw capercaille among the splendid stands of Caledonian pines in Glen Affric.

A camp near the Alltbeithe Youth Hostel in Glen Affric with Paul Hawksworth and a party of boys in November 1972. Three perfect days of autumn sunshine with only hoar frost and a sprinkling of new snow on the high ridges.

A traverse of Sgurr nan Ceathreamhnan up east ridge and down south ridge. 5 hours.

An Socach, Mam Sodhail and Carn Eige from the col west of An Socach. Many ptarmigan on the ridge, the odd snow bunting and a dark brown fox among the rocks near the summit of Mam Sodhail. 8 hours.

From the road bridge at the end of Loch Beinn a' Mheadhoin a superb round of Tom a' Choinich, Carn Eige and Mam Sodhail, returning down the long south-east ridge over Sgurr na Lapaich can be made quite easily. In early August 1981 my wife and I, plus 12-year-old daughter Lucy, accomplished it in 8 hours.

A stalker's path runs up Glen nam Fiadh to the bealach under Toll Creagach, then a pleasant ridge, rocky in places, continues to the summit of Tom a' Choinich. Another long and winding ridge leads to Carn Eige and Mam Sodhail.

This was my first summer visit to the range and I was in no way disappointed. The Glen Affric peaks are amongst my favourite in all Scotland, with their considerable height, remoteness, broad ridges and steep north-facing corries. On this day the glens were teeming with deer, while on the tops we saw eagles, buzzards and mountain hares.

In by-gone days this must have been an extremely well-run estate. The stalkers' paths are still, mainly, in good repair, thanks to efficient and long-lasting drainage, and on the high ridge between Tom a' Choinich and Carn Eige proper stone steps have been constructed in steep places.

We found a visitors' book by the cairn on Mam Sodhail which we duly signed before leaving for Sgurr na Lapaich and Glen Affric.

CHAPTER 14

Alltbeithe

A'CHRALAIG 3673ft/1120m
MULLACH FRAOCH-CHOIRE 3614ft/1102m
BEINN FHIONNLAIDH (Ross-shire) 3294ft/1005m
MULLACH NA DHEIRAGAIN 3210ft/982m
BEN ATTOW (FHADA) 3383ft/1032m

3 July 1970 My brother Christopher, Paul Hawksworth and I left Cluanie Inn at 10.30 a.m. carrying bivouac gear and food for three days. We climbed directly but steeply to the summit of A'Chralaig. The clouds were above the tops and we had occasional sunshine. Continuing to Mullach Fraoch-choire, we enjoyed a razor-sharp ridge near this peak's summit. A golden eagle swooped down to examine us. To the north Sgurr nan Ceathreamhnan blocked the view, to the west was the shapely peak of Ciste Dhubh. To the east stretched Loch Affric and to the south appeared range after range of mountains; the Cluanie Forest peaks, the Loch Quoich peaks, the Loch Arkaig peaks and the Glenfinnan peaks. There were still extensive patches of snow in the north-facing corries.

We scrambled down steep slopes on the north side of Mullach Fraoch-choire and waded the river Affric. It was knee deep. It was 1.30 p.m. and lunch time.

Our next objective was the far distant Beinn Fhionnlaidh which I had missed out when walking across the Mam Sodhail range in March 1962. It lies one-and-a-half miles north of Carn Eige overlooking Loch Mullardoch. We climbed up to the Bealach Coire Ghaidheil and then made a long (2½ hour) traverse of the western slopes of Mam Sodhail and Carn Eige. We reached the summit of Beinn Fhionnlaidh at 8 p.m. Tired now, we dropped down to Gleann a' Choilich, cooked supper and bivouacked.

4 July 1970   It started to rain in the early hours and by morning we were pretty wet. After a hasty breakfast, we climbed up to the Creag a' Coire Aird ridge and, in steady drizzle and cloud, walked along towards Sgurr nan Ceathreamhnan. We passed Loch Coire nan Dearcag and crossing the ridge, dropped down to Glen Affric for lunch. I startled a hen ptarmigan and her brood. It was a wet blustery day but between the showers the wind nearly dried us out only for us to be soaked again a few minutes later. Christopher was having serious trouble with his feet. He had forgotten to bring his boots on this three-day backpacking expedition and had managed this far in an old pair of klets which we found in the boot of my car. The klets were now falling apart. We made for the Camban bothy under Ciste Dhubh and found it dry, for it had recently been renovated by the Mountain Bothies Association.

At 3 p.m. lying on the floor in a sleeping bag was a bearded Scot, a professional bothymonger. He lived in mountain bothies during the summer months and we were given a long list of places in Scotland where you could get a good doss. We collected bog-wood from some way off and with difficulty lit a fire to get dry by. Our bearded friend emerged from his bag and sat unmoving right over the fire. He stayed there late into the night until the ashes were finally cold.

After tea I left the others and made a very enjoyable ascent of Ben Attow up the east ridge. Camban bothy to the summit in 2 hours. It was good to be free of my rucksack for once. The day cleared up and I had sunshine and views down to Loch Duich. The northern corries of Ben Attow were grand and still full of snow. On my way back, I found a meadow pippet's nest with five eggs.

We left the bothy at 6.30 a.m. the following day in steady rain and 2 hours 20 minutes later reached Cluanie Inn.

On a sunny day in November 1972, when there was only a light powdering of snow on the tops, I ascended Ben Attow by the east ridge from a camp near Alltbeithe. Back down the north-east ridge to Loch a' Bhealaich, thence Alltbeithe. Huge herds of deer grazing the southern slopes of Sgurr nan Ceathreamhnan. 5 hours.

CHAPTER 15

Cluanie and Glen Shiel

AONACH MEADHOIN (SGURR AN FHUARAIL) 3284ft/1003m
SGURR A' BHEALAICH DHEIRG 3378ft/1038m
SAILEAG 3124ft/959m
SGURR NA CISTE DUIBHE 3370ft/1027m
SGURR FHUARAN 3505ft/1068m

3 April 1969 Oliver, his wife Daphne, and I were off
from Cluanie at 8.50 a.m. bound for the long ridge of
mountains north of Glen Shiel – the celebrated Five
Sisters of Kintail. I felt very unfit on the steep south
ridge of Aonach Meadhoin on the Sgurr an Fhuarail
massif. The clouds were down to 2,500ft and we had a
horrid squall of sleet which lasted nearly 2 hours.

The wind-blown snow had made the broadest ridges
into snow arêtes. The rocky ridge leading to the cairn
on Sgurr a' Bhealaich Dheirg was buried in powder-
snow and was quick tricky.

As the day went on the weather improved and at 1.15
p.m. we sat in sunshine on the low col to the west of
Saileag. We were directly above our camp in Glen Shiel
and we could see the tents. The temptation proved too
much for Daphne who returned to camp, but Oliver
and I pressed on over Sgurr na Ciste Duibhe to Sgurr
Fhuaran. The ridge involved much ascent and descent
and below the 3,000ft level the snow was sugary and let
us in over our boots. However, as we proceeded, the
weather became magnificent, a cold wind but sunny with

tremendous views in all directions.

At 4 p.m. we had a long rest in the sun on Sgurr Fhuaran, the highest of the Five Sisters. We could just catch the aroma of wood-smoke from heather burning far below. We quickly descended 3,300ft off the west ridge, running down the last part through the heather to immerse our heads in a burn and to drink our fill.

We managed to cross the River Shiel dry-shod by traversing an alder branch to reach an island then by sloth-like climbing along a branch of another tree to the opposite bank. No sooner had we reached the road than a car driven by an old friend stopped and ran us back to camp. He had been on his way back from Skye and had recognised us. A great day indeed.

CISTE DHUBH 3218ft/982m

2 April 1969 It was a raw overcast day and I set off alone for Ciste Dhubh. I followed the Cluanie-Alltbeithe track for two-and-a-half miles and then climbed up a steep shoulder to the south ridge. The snow was steep and I had to surmount a small cornice to gain the ridge. The ridge itself was very icy with long drops to either side and a cornice to the east. I found it distinctly nasty and it took an hour of step-cutting to reach the summit. I should have worn crampons.

To the north of the cairn the plateau was a sheet of ice and I began to wonder how I could get off the mountain. I cut steps towards the north-west shoulder and was able to descend to the glen above Camban bothy. I had to reascend over Bealach a' Choinich to regain the Alltbeithe track but I was back at Cluanie at 3.15 p.m. There was no sun and the clouds, though thin, covered the tops.

A'GHLAS-BHEINN 3006ft/918m
CREAG NAN DAMH 3012ft/918m
SGURR AN LOCHAIN 3282ft/1004m
SGURR AN DOIRE LEATHAIN 3272ft/1010m

27 March 1967   There was a late but heavy snowfall
in Scotland in 1967. Driving over Rannoch Moor Oliver
and I counted seven cars off the road either upside-
down or in the ditch. After camping for the night on
snow beside the road at Cluanie the next day was sleety
and overcast. We drove down to Loch Shiel and from
Dorusduain made a quick ascent of A'Ghlas-bheinn.
There was wet snow by Loch Shiel but higher up it was
deep and powdery. We were up and down in 3 hours as
the weather did not encourage us to linger and there
was no view.

28 March 1967   All night long heavy sleet showers and
strong winds buffeted the tent and we needed rocks on
the pegs and snow-flap to keep it down. By 9.30 a.m.
patches of blue sky were appearing and we drove down
the glen to the Glen Shiel battle site. We struck up the
northern shoulder of Creag nan Damh but were soon in
deep powder-snow. The going was very hard and it
took us 3 hours of strenuous floundering to reach the
summit. Where possible we took to the rocks, but only
the largest boulders were above the snow and it was an
almost completely white world. I have never seen such
quanties of snow in Britain. At best we were knee-deep
and at worst waist-deep.

As we climbed up the weather closed in and it was
snowing steadily. On the summit the wind was blowing
snow particles with great force and at times we could
not see anything. On the ridge however there were odd
patches of clear ground, the snow having been blown

off. We traversed the ridge over Sgurr an Lochain to Sgurr an Doire Leathain in high wind, snow and deteriorating conditions. Our lunch stop was ruined by our untouched cold whole chicken, complete in polythene bag, tobogganing down the southern slopes out of sight into the mist.

We retreated down the northern spur of Sgurr an Doire Leathain. The waist-deep snow persisted practically to the road.

Later we dried out in front of a good fire in the bar of the Cluanie Inn while the blizzard continued to rage outside.

CARN GHLUASAID 3140ft/957m
SGURR NAN CONBHAIREAN 3635ft/1110m
SAIL CHAORAINN 3285ft/1002m

1 April 1969 Oliver, Daphne and I left the car near Lundie ruin by Loch Cluanie and were off before 9 a.m. We struck straight up the hillside on to Carn Ghluasaid. The summit plateau was in bright sunshine and there were superb views. It was a day of sun and snow. We could see the snowstorms coming but they never lasted very long and were always followed by bright skies.

We followed the ridge north-west on to the imposing snow peak of Sgurr nan Conbhairean. It had a circle of cliffs to the north-east, corniced and plastered with snow. Our next objective Tigh Mor lay a mile north of Sgurr nan Conbhairean and we had to continue beyond the summit before we could find descendable snow slopes leading to grassy Glen na Ciche 2000ft below. At 1.15 we had a leisurely lunch by the burn in warm sunshine.

We had intended to climb the sharp peak of Mullach Fraoch-choire and to traverse the ridge to A' Chralaig. However, our way to the summit involved a sharp exposed ridge, the east ridge, which was corniced and rocky. The snow was so poor and we had no rope, so, only 200ft from the top of Mullach Fraoch-choire, we decided to retreat. We descended into the north corrie and crossed the north-west ridge before reaching the bealach between Cluanie and Alltbeithe. Three miles of bog and rough track led us to the main road and we were back at the car at 7.30 p.m.

CREAG A' MHAIM 3102ft/947m
DRUIM SHIONNACH 3222ft/987m
AONACH AIR CHRITH 3342ft/1021m
MAOL CHINN-DEARG 3214ft/981m

30 March 1967   Oliver and I set off at 9 a.m. from the locked gates on the old Cluanie–Tomdoun road about a mile beyond the causeway over Loch Cluanie. There was very deep snow, but we were surprised to find in the two days since we had done the western sections of the Cluanie ridge that some of the snow had frozen enough to take our weight. After 2 hours we emerged into bright sunshine on top of Creag a' Mhaim. There was little wind and the views were stupendous. Across Glen Loyne to the south the nearby, snow-plastered, Spidean Mialach was particularly impressive.

Ten minutes later we were in mist on a compass bearing with snow swirling around. It was that type of day, typically Scottish and exhilarating. The ridges were heavily-corniced and at times plumed to a razor.

We traversed Druim Shionnach and continued to Aonach air Chrith. On the final ridge of this mountain we saw an extraordinary phenomenon. The high wind had blown the powdery snow in an upwards motion against the ridge forming fantastic plumes of snow 30–50ft high.

Luckily the leeward slope was not too steep so we could traverse underneath the overhanging plumes.

We continued to the 3214ft summit of Maol Chinn-dearg and the clouds rolled back and the position provided the climax of the day. We could easily see Ladhar Bheinn and Sgurr na Ciche to the west. An easy descent down the north ridge led us to the road in 55 minutes, luckily most of this ridge had been swept clear of snow.

We walked back to the car and had tea at Cluanie Inn as once again snow swept down Glen Shiel.

BEN SGRITHEALL (SGRIOL) 3196ft/974m

9 August 1964 On a wet and miserable day *en route* for Skye I drove round to Arnisdale and ascended Ben Sgriol. A 2¾ hour trip up and down. Straight up from Arnisdale the slopes are steep grass and scree although there is a band of rocks at the top.

The midges were terrible and I got a score or more bites while changing out of my wet socks.

THE SADDLE 3317ft/1010m
SGURR NA SGINE 3098ft/945m

10 August 1964 From a camp site in Glen Shiel. The Saddle has a lot of character and I enjoyed the steep and rocky ridge on the east side. The summit ridge too was narrow and airy. The views south were extensive and included Sgurr na Ciche and Ladhar Bheinn. To the west were the Cuillins. The sun was hot but I found a cool lochan on the bealach leading to Sgurr na Sgine. This latter mountain forms a horseshoe with Faochag and I continued the walk round to Faochag's summit before descending steeply to camp again. 4 hours hard going.

I climbed the Saddle again in August 1971 with Paul Hawksworth. We had had very poor weather on Skye and were determined to have at least one good day out on the way back.

At Shiel Bridge the clouds parted slightly so we set off for the Saddle. The lull was temporary and for the next 5 hours we were caught in a tremendous gale of wind and rain that left the burns raging white and flooded the river Shiel over its banks.

We walked up beside the Allt Undalain, ascending corrie after corrie, each with its rocky lip and waterfall. We passed Loch a' Choir'Uaine and scrambled steeply up on to Spidean Dhomhuill Bhric. The Saddle traverse was exciting, a sharp ridge exposed on each side and we were buffeted constantly by the squalls of heavy rain. We continued beyond the true summit due east over another narrow ridge and then down Coire Mhalagain to the road. We had to pick our descent carefully as crossing the burns was still quite difficult high up. Low down they would have been impossible.

CHAPTER 16

Loch Quoich
and Loch Lochay

GLEOURAICH 3395ft/1035m
SPIDEAN MIALACH 3268ft/996m
SGURR A' MHAORAICH 3365ft/1027m

17 December 1970 With Paul Hawksworth. A full
gale was howling down Glen Garry as we drove in the
evening towards Loch Quoich. We could only drive
slowly as the wipers were unable to cope with the
lashing rain, and I was reminded of my previous visit to
this area in similar conditions in March 1963.

We stopped for a drink at the Tomdoun Hotel and
the kind proprietress allowed us to sleep in our sleeping
bags on comfortable beds for the night, although the
hotel was closed for residents in the winter.

The next morning we found the bad weather had
moved on and we had an excellent day of strong winds,
showers of hail and sunshine. The hills above 2,000ft
were white with fresh snow.

We left the car parked near the site of the submerged
Glenquoich Lodge and traversed Gleouraich and
Spidean Mialach in a round trip of 4¼ hours. There is a
well-constructed stalkers path leading up on to the summit ridge of Gleouraich. Loch Quoich looked almost
friendly with the sun on it, and we had good views of the
Cluanie Peaks and Gairich. We saw a golden eagle.

18 December 1970 We camped for the night at Kinlochhourn but the weather closed in and next morning it was raining with the clouds right down. We left the car near Loch a' Choire Bheithe at 9.30 a.m., when it was still quite dark, and made a wet and cold ascent of Sgurr a' Mhaoraich by the easy south ridge. Back by 12 noon.

It was a pity we had such poor conditions, as Sgurr a' Mhaoraich looks an attractive mountain in a remote and beautiful area.

GAIRICH 3015ft/919m
SGURR MOR (Loch Quoich) 3290ft/1003m

3 April 1971 With Paul Hawksworth and a party of boys from Ampleforth College. We left Loch Quoich dam at 8 a.m. and walked up the east ridge of Gairich. It is a fine mountain with bluffs of rock on the ridge and is a good view point. We had a superb sunny day with verglas on the rocks early on and just a powdering of fresh snow.

We descended to Coire Ghlais and traversed just below the summit of Sgurr an Fhuarain to reach the col under Sgurr Mor. This latter peak looked imposing with snow-covered crags on three sides and from the summit we could make out Sgurr na Ciche and Ladhar Bheinn. While we were sitting by the cairn having our lunch a lone figure with an ice-axe appeared up the west ridge. He had walked over from Loch Arkaig. We ran down the slopes to upper Glen Kingie and lay down enjoying the warm sunshine. We watched a fox making his way up the slopes behind us and a pair of eagles surveyed us from above. It was a long, long walk back down Glen Kingie – nine miles to the da – and we were not back at camp until 5 p.m. I have very happy memories of this day, perhaps because Sgurr Mor was my penultimate Munro.

MEALL NA TEANGA 3050ft/917m
SRON A' CHOIRE GHAIRBH 3066ft/935m

17 August 1966   From Kilfinnan on Loch Lochay. An hour's walk through the extensive forestry plantation led me to a good path ascending to the col under Meall Dubh. The heather was just coming out and there was a profusion of flowers and bilberries on the lower slopes. The day was fine and I had a pleasant and leisurely day.

I climbed the easy slopes to the west of Meall Dubh leading to the summit of Meall na Teanga and then returned to the col and climbed Sron a' Choire Ghairbh. All round there were extensive views as these two Munros have no near neighbours.

I descended the east ridge over Sean Mheall direct to Kilfinnan having been out 6 hours.

CHAPTER 17

Knoydart

LADHAR BHEINN 3343ft/1020m
LUINNE BHEINN 3083ft/939m
MEALL BUIDHE (Loch Nevis) 3107ft/946m
SGURR NA CICHE 3410ft/1040m
SGURR NAN COIREACHAN (Glen Dessarry) 3125ft/953m

With my wife Trisha and Alan and Janet Wedgwood. We left Kinlochhourn with tents and food for four days and plodded our way to Barrisdale. It was a fine and sunny day and the scenery was magnificent with steep mountainsides falling straight into Loch Hourn. We passed delightful inlets and deserted cottages at Skiary and Runival. At Barrisdale there is a large shooting lodge with farm attached, supplied by boat from Arnisdale across Loch Hourn. Smoke was coming out of a cottage chimney and dogs barked but we saw nobody.

We camped on a spit of grass the far side of the stream and cooked supper over a driftwood fire. The evening sun lit up the surrounding hills and Ben Sgriol across the loch, deer grazed near by; the place was enchanting and still.

22 March 1963 The next day was warm and the sun shone from a cloudless sky. We traversed Ladhar Bheinn returning to camp by mid afternoon. The 3,400ft from sea level took us 3½ hours with rests in the sun. Our eyes were continually drawn down to the blue

Loch Hourn and Ben Sgriol. We went up the north-east ridge, Druim a Choire Odhair, and after traversing the sharp snowy summit ridge descended over Aonach Sgoilte and the steep Creag Bheithe. Back in camp, Alan and Janet bathed in the loch; it was really summer weather.

At 4 p.m. we shouldered our packs and struck up Glen Unndalain towards Luinne Bheinn. At 6 p.m. we found an idyllic camp site by a stream on a platform of grass at the 2,200ft level. Our view was down the glen to Loch Hourn and the west. That evening there was a tremendous sunset reflecting the hills in the loch. Even late at night the western sky was alight with a greenish glow. We were startled by a falling star seeming so near that it must hit us. After supper we breached the whisky.

23 March 1963 The next day was a long one in very wild and rugged country. We traversed Luinne Bheinn in mist; left our rucksacks on the bealach under the southern slopes and then climbed Meall Buidhe. Back at the bealach, we had a long descent down a wild corrie to Carnoch, practically at sea-level at the head of Loch Nevis.

The sun came out for a spell and we basked and had tea before attempting the 2,500ft steep ascent to the south-west ridge of Sgurr na Ciche. A pair of golden eagles paid us a fleeting visit.

The climb was hot and exhausting, and we made a detour to drink at a waterfall where we disturbed a herd of deer. On the ridge the weather was ominous, so we camped for the night. Mist swirled around but we had occasional glimpses of the sharp summit of Sgurr na Ciche only 1,000ft above us. It was 5.30 p.m.

Life was at its very best. We finished off the whisky

and had a last round of liar dice. Only an easy day lay between us and the car and our pre-booked dinner at the Tomdoun Hotel. It was with a clear conscience that we polished off our last main meal and settled down to sleep.

24 March 1963   We woke early to the sound of rain and wind buffeting the tents. We quickly packed up our already sodden equipment, forewent breakfast and continued up the ridge in swirling mist. The gale was increasing every minute. The rocks were verglassed and dangerous and several times we were forced to find alternative routes. It was difficult to look ahead with our faces covered by gloved hands as protection from the driving sleet.

Quite suddenly we were at the summit trig point where we held a counsel of war behind a rock. Our next Munro was two miles away but according to our map virtually *en route* to the car – we decided to press on. It took 2 hours to gain the col 600ft below the summit of Sgurr nan Coireachan. The traverse had been a nightmare. Horizontal sleet driven by an 80 m.p.h. gale had pounded us the whole way and we were soaked and frozen. We fought our way to the summit of the mountain, much of the time on hands and knees, crawling from rock to rock and hanging on with numbed hands. Conversation was impossible. It was this col that was crossed by Bonnie Prince Charlie at midnight on 19 July 1746.

After dropping down from the summit the wind eased somewhat but the rain poured down unabated. Trisha fell into the Allt a' Choire Reidh while crossing it and was completely submerged, but it made little difference and for once humour was lacking.

To our astonishment we arrived at Loch Quoich side.

Our map did not show the dam and the resulting two or three mile westward extension of the loch. To attain the causeway at the west end of Loch Quoich we had either to negotiate exhausting moraines or to wade knee-deep through mud and ooze by the water's edge. With our leaden packs we chose the latter.

At 1.30 p.m., after wading waist deep through a burn we got on to a good track leading along the north side of the loch in the direction of the car. This was the old shooting path made before the loch level was raised and thus, at frequent intervals, it would disappear into the loch and we would have steep trackless hillside to traverse instead.

The rain was incessant. None of us have seen rain like it before or since. It swept down in curtains and the hillsides were white with water.

We were only four miles from the Kinlochhourn road when, rounding a hummock, we saw the Amhain Cosaidh burn ahead. It was a foaming, roaring torrent fully 50 yards across, hurtling into Loch Quoich. The top branches of trees were sticking out of the water in places and beyond, tantalisingly, we could see our path continuing. It was 3.00 p.m.

We hoped that by striking up Glen Cosaidh alongside the burn we would soon be able to cross. Some hope! The glen above was turned into a lake and beyond that the water swept on. The rain never eased, our packs bore us down and we were nearly exhausted. Our last gingerbread had sufficed for breakfast and lunch some hours before.

The minor burns flowing down into the main one now became major obstacles and often entailed wading up to our waists. At 6.00 p.m. we were some miles up the corrie and the burn divided. The mountainside

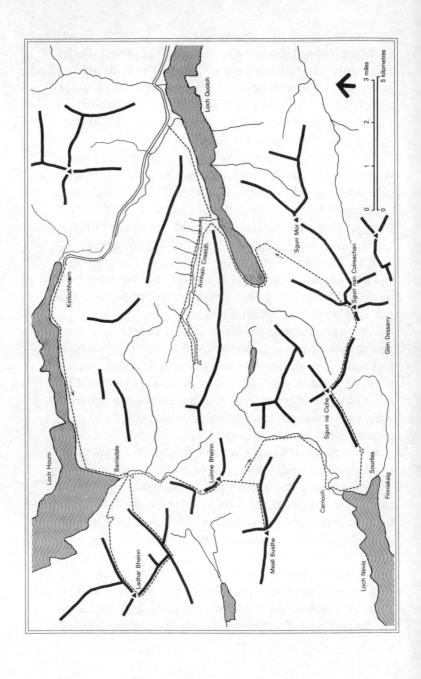

became steeper but the left-hand branch was still unfordable; it roared down in a torrent of foam. A stag swam across ahead of us with just its horns visible above the water.

At 7 p.m., safeguarded by the rope, Alan managed to cross the left-hand branch. Janet followed but was swept away only to be 'played' to the bank by Alan. They advised us not to follow.

We staggered on up the corrie. Alan and Janet recrossed over to Trisha and myself and we decided to camp where we were as it was nearly dark.

Somehow we got a tent up in the gale. Pegs were useless in the sodden ground and we put huge boulders on the guys. Even so the guy ropes were snapping at intervals like cotton. We lay exhausted in our sodden bags knowing that once the tent went our position would be desperate indeed.

It was a hellish night and only Janet slept at all. Water was entering the tent all the time and we were shivering uncontrollably.

By morning the wind and rain had eased and we struggled into our dripping clothes again. We were desperately hungry and weak, but managed to cross both branches of the burn easily now and eventually reached the track again. We all suffered from raw rubbed thighs and feet from our wet clothing and our hands were peeling. However, some hours later the lost dinner was made up for twofold in Fort William. We can now understand why Kinlochquoich boasts a record average rainfall of 159 inches per annum. Indeed Professor Gordon Manley in his book *Climate and the British Scene* reckons that the rainfall in the high glens west of Loch Quoich could average over 200 inches per annum.

In April 1970, I returned to Barrisdale with Paul Hawksworth and a party of schoolboys. We chartered a boat from Mallaig to Inverie from Mr. MacLeod the boatman from the Dr. Barnardo's holiday house at remote Camusrory by Loch Nevis. We were met at Inverie by an irate man, the Factor of the Estate. However, he was pleased to hear we were going to Barrisdale which is not his responsibility.

For four days we had cold and wintry weather. Fresh snow fell every night. We ascended Ladhar Bheinn from the east but the steep Creag Bheithe defeated us and we had to climb an easier way to the bealach below the summit. The high ridges were corniced and quite tricky and we decided to descend by the broad and easy north-west ridge rather than attempt to hit off the narrow north-east ridge in the thick mist. A 9 hour day.

The following day we walked back to Inverie and were lucky enough to see a golden eagle being harried by a pair of hawks.

In November 1976 I took a party to Knoydart to stay in Finniskaig cottage beside Loch Nevis. After an eight-mile walk-in from Glen Dessarry Lodge, carrying huge loads, we arrived at the river's edge in near darkness, but the outline of the gable-end was just discernible against the sky.

'We'll soon have you warm and dry', I shouted to the boys who began wading the swift stream. But, to my horror, Finniskaig was a ruin and completely derelict.

Using some rusty roofing sheets we managed to construct a lean-to shelter, but at 5.30 a.m. squalls of rain began driving down the glen and soaking our sleeping bags. We packed up our belongings, donned waterproofs and, by torch light, fought our way against the gale back into Upper Glen Dessarry and the shelter of A'Chuil bothy. In the conditions, the Loch Nevis to A'Chuil walk took 3½ hours.

From A'Chuil we climbed Sgurr nan Coireachan, which is easily accessible to the north of the glen, and also walked along the hummocky connecting ridge to Sgurr na Ciche. For the second time on this remote mountain the weather was bad and there was no view. From the col on the east side of Sgurr na Ciche a narrow gully leads down to Mam na Cloich Airde and provides an extremely rapid return route to Upper Glen Dessarry. From A'Chuil to Sgurr na Ciche via Garbh Chioch Mhor and back to A'Chuil took 5¾ hours.

Yet another approach to remote Knoydart is by sea from Mallaig to the head of Loch Nevis. In November 1979, with Gerard Simpson and some boys, we persuaded Tom Maclean (the ex SAS man who has twice made record single-handed crossings of the Atlantic, and who now runs an Outdoor Activities Centre at Tarbet) to take us to Sourlies bothy in his boat *Gipsy Rover*.

Sourlies provides an excellent base for an ascent of Sgurr na Ciche up the south-west ridge. This route, combined with a descent south down the scree gully from the Sgurr na Ciche, Garbh Chioch Mhor bealach took 5½ hours in bad weather.

A warning note for would-be inhabitants of Sourlies that fire wood, even drift wood, is in short supply. On the other hand the mussels are prolific and delicious.

CHAPTER 18

Glenfinnan

GAOR BHEINN (GULVAIN) 3224ft/987m
SGURR THUILM 3164ft/963m
SGURR NAN COIREACHAN (Glenfinnan) 3133ft/956m

I was staying at the Stage House Inn, Glenfinnan, as a guest on the spring meet of the Scottish Mountaineering Club.

17 April 1965   I teamed up with Stanley Thomson and W. H. (Bill) Murray and on a grey raw day we walked up Glen Fionnlighe to Gulvain. There was snow on the high ridge connecting the north and south summits, but in general I thought it a rather featureless and isolated mountain. We found a baited gin-trap which we threw into a deep pool and we investigated what appeared to be a sheep stuck on a ledge of a cliff. The sheep turned out to be dead; it had hanged itself in a forked branch of a tree jutting out from a rock.

18 April 1965   The weather was still overcast and threatening the next day. I set out with Thomson and others to do the Sgurr Thuilm–Sgurr nan Coireachan horseshoe at the head of Glenfinnan. The blizzard broke when we were high up on the south ridge of Sgurr Thuilm. We struggled to the summit cairn in a white-out with raging sleet accompanied by thunder and lightning. The wind-blown sleet stung our heads even through balaclava and anorak hood and, at times, we had to crouch down with gloved hands over our faces for protection. We turned about and hastened down the mountain again. At the 1,000ft level the hail turned to rain. This area of Scotland was certainly living up to its reputation for bad weather. The annual rainfall at Glenfinnan is 120 inches.

Back at the hotel we learned that Bill Murray and W. M. Mackenzie who were on Sgurr nan Coireachan had been thrown to the ground by lightning striking the ridge thirty feet away. They could smell the sulphurous fumes of burning rock, and Mackenzie suffered burns on the soles of his feet.

19 April 1965 Although the meet now broke up I stayed on an extra day to climb Sgurr nan Coireachan. Up Glenfinnan on a much improved day, and then the south-east ridge of the mountain from Corryhully. I was impressed by the mountain; the ridge was interesting as much snow had fallen in the last two days. The sun shone through gaps in the clouds and I had glimpses of the Sgurr na Ciche range to the north. I returned the same way. 5 hours the round trip from the hotel.

In November 1976 I climbed Sgurr Thuilm from A'Chuil bothy in Glen Dessarry. The ridge south of A'Chuil has to be climbed and then descended into Glen Pean and we discovered that the hills had been fenced prior to planting. We met a stalker with rifle and ponies who was clearing the entire area of game, shooting everything that moved. At Glen Pean bothy we waded the river and then tackled the steep northern slopes of Sgurr Thuilm.

The sky was darkening minute by minute and the wind was swinging round to the south-west and freshening. The long Sgurr na Ciche, Sgurr Mor ridge was silhouetted to the north, while westwards we could see down Loch Nevis.

This is a bleak area which suffers almost continuous bad weather and today was no exception. Inevitably, the rain started soon after we left the summit cairn and it drove us down the mountain towards Strathan. Luckily we found a bridge over the river Pean and we rounded the ridge into Glen Dessarry. A'Chuil was reached at 5 p.m., just as the light was fading, after a 7-hour expedition.

An old man, a bothymonger, was crouched over the fire and he had burned most of our wood. He was the same man that had burned our wood in Camban bothy in 1970. There was nothing for it but to brave the elements again and search the saturated hillsides for old heather roots and bog wood.

CHAPTER 19

Skye

SGURR NAN GILLEAN 3167ft/965m
AM BASTEIR 3050ft/935m
BRUACH NA FRITHE 3143ft/958m
SGURR DEARG (INACCESSIBLE PINNACLE) 3254ft/986m
SGURR MHIC COINNICH 3107ft/948m
SGURR NAN EAG 3037ft/924m
SGURR DUBH MOR 3089ft/944m
SGURR ALASDAIR 3309ft/993m
SGURR NA BANACHDICH 3167ft/965m
SGURR A'GHREADAIDH 3197ft/973m
SGURR A'MHADAIDH 3014ft/918m
BLAVEN 3042ft/928m

In September 1958, to celebrate my demobilisation from the army after National Service, Oliver and I hitched up to Skye for a few days. We were standing beside the road in Glen Garry, waving our thumbs, when a chauffeur-driven Rolls-Royce drew up beside us and gave us a lift. Sitting in the back was Dame Flora MacLeod of MacLeod who shared her lunch of cold chicken and white wine with us as we sped to Sligachan. We camped in Glen Sligachan and started off with two damp days when we were devoured by midges. All the stories you hear about the savagery of Skye midges are true. We had an old tent with loose entrance and no sewn in groundsheet and the inside of the tent soon became literally black with midges. Cooking was a nightmare, with the soup being covered in midges and midges entering our noses, ears and mouths making us choke. However the weather improved and we enjoyed two days of brilliant sun and hot weather.

6 September 1958   The classic Pinnacle Ridge of Sgurr nan Gillean was our first introduction to Cuillin gabbro and we were thrilled by the experience. On a warm summer's day this hard rough rock must give the best climbing anywhere. We climbed the first pinnacle by the Black Chimney route and then continued up the normal Pinnacle Ridge route to the pointed summit of Sgurr nan Gillean. The route is not hard but it provided us with an airy introduction to the ridges of the Black Cuillin.

8 September 1958   On another day we climbed the Bhasteir Tooth by the North Chimney (Shadbolt's Climb) and we found this exciting as it includes a 40ft back-and-knee pitch and finally a tunnel leading to the actual summit of the tooth. We felt very pleased with ourselves sitting in the sun having lunch on the Tooth, we were not very experienced rock climbers and from our campsite the Tooth looked excessively difficult and exposed, jutting out fang-like from the ridge in sharp silhouette.

We continued along the ridge westward to Bruach na Frithe but no further. It was a scorching hot day and, mad with thirst, we fled to a deep pool in a Glen Sligachan stream and swam and drank our fill.

It was on this holiday that we found ourselves in Fort William at 2 a.m. while hitching south. We walked up the pony track to the summit of Ben Nevis to see the sunrise only to be greeted by a cold wind and swirling mists.

In August of the following year Christopher and I camped in Glen Brittle for two nights. The weather was bad and the rocks were wet.

28 August 1959   We walked up to Sron na Ciche and climbed Cioch Direct which was a thoroughly good route and we enjoyed it in spite of the the conditions. We then climbed the upper buttress by the Crack of Doom which had something of a reputation in those days. We were in practice and did not find it too hard. The top pitch was the crux with water running down the crack. The combination of these two climbs had been described as '. . . perhaps the finest day's mountaineering in Britain' and in 1919 Meldrum and Bower wrote: 'This was the sort of climb one vows never to revisit, except in nightmares.'

The weather cleared up in the afternoon and we had views of Rhum and Eigg from the summit of Sgumain. Having descended into upper Coire Lagan we decided the day was young so we traversed across the Alasdair Stone Shoot and then climbed up again to Bealach Mhic Coinnich from whence a scramble took us to the cairn on Sgurr Mhic Coinnich. We descended via the north ridge and Bealach Coire Lagan.

29 August 1959   The next day was cold and wet. We walked up to Sgurr Dearg and the Inaccessible Pinnacle. It looked impressive and hard in the mist and I certainly found the steep west ridge quite difficult with numbed fingers. It was not a day to be on the Cuillin Ridge so we abseiled off the top and retreated to Glen Brittle.

In August 1964 Trisha and I and our first born, Timothy, aged 10 weeks, were staying at Glen Brittle Post Office. My brother Oliver was camping at Loch an Fhirbhallaich and eating fresh trout every night. The weather was superb so we decided to have an attempt on the Skye Ridge.

12 August 1964   We left the tent at 6.15 a.m. and had

a very tedious traverse of Coires Lagan, Ghrunnda and Laogh before climbing steeply up Gars-bheinn. Rhum and Canna were wreathed in mists and it was already hot at 7.00 a.m. We left Gars-bheinn summit at 9.15 a.m. with wisps of cloud hanging over Loch Coruisk and Sgurr nan Gillean, our final objective, looking invitingly near.

Our water bottle held only one pint and as there is no supply on the ridge it soon became clear that drastic rationing would be required. It was incredibly hot, the rocks were hot to touch and there was not a breath of wind. We moved very slowly, savouring any shade that we found. We made a detour of 30 minutes to take in the summit of Sgurr Dubh Mor and allowed ourselves one mouthful of water for our pains.

At 12.30 we sat in the Thearlaich-Dubh gap and had some lunch, but our throats were too dry to eat anything except an apple. I found the ascent out of the gap very awkward even when second on the rope; it was the first rock climbing I'd done for over a year. At 1.30 p.m. we were on Sgurr Alasdair with the water bottle empty. We proceeded slowly, moving like ghosts, over Mhic Coinnich and An Stac where we gave up. In five minutes we had descended the fast screes to Loch Lagan where we lazed, splashed and cooled off.

The hot weather had drained us of our enthusiasm and drive and thirst won the day.

14 August 1964   A few days later I set out alone up Sgurr nan Gobhar, the peak at the end of the Banachdich ridge which overlooks Glen Brittle. It was a misty morning and from Sgurr Banachdich summit I saw a fine Brocken Spectre. All round the Cuillin peaks were jutting up into the blue sky from a bed of cloud at the 2,000ft level. It is always a magnificent spectacle when this occurs and there is no better place to see it than the Cuillins.

I continued along the sharp exposed ridge over Ghreadaidh and Mhadaidh in a world of my own. I saw no one else on this stretch of the ridge. Back to Glen Brittle down Coire Ghreadaidh.

16 August 1964   Two days later the weather broke and Oliver and I drove round to Elgol. We walked alongside Loch Scavaig to Camasunary and climbed Blaven by the south-west ridge. The surrounding peaks looked particularly awe-inspiring rising into the mists with storm clouds glowering overhead.

Once we had attained the ridge Blaven made an easy climb but it was a pity there was no view. We descended the scree gully between the peaks and found a more direct route to Elgol than descending to Camasunary first. A 5 hour round trip from Elgol.

In November 1976 I was staying at the Glen Brittle Memorial Hut with a school party and we had just climbed the Inaccessible Pinnacle, the most technically difficult Munro. But, having all abseiled down to the screes again, the rope, which I had passed round a huge detached block, became well and truly jammed. We all heaved and hauled and eventually pulled the block clean off its plinth; it landed amongst us and thundered down the screes towards Loch Lagan. A very lucky escape.

Later that week we climbed Sgurr nan Gillean on a still, autumn day that was warm and sunny. We lingered on the summit drinking in the view that stretched from the Outer Isles to An Teallach and from Ben Nevis to Ben More on Mull. Mindful of my inexperienced charges I secured a rope across the famous *gendarme* on the west ridge, for protection. I was glad that I did, for there was quite a bit of doubt and slithering from some of the party.

Skye weather seems to come in extremes. In August 1981 our long awaited holiday, when I would introduce my wife and four children to Coruisk, arrived. MacKinnon, the Elgol boatman, took us in to the Coruisk Memorial Hut for a four-day stay. Four days of continuous gales and lashing rain which virtually cut us off, because both the Scavaig River and the Mad Burn were impassable.

We took some solice, drinking gins and tonics in the snug cabins of luxury yachts that had sought shelter in the inner recesses of Loch na Cuilce. Other diversions were watching the salmon leaping up the falls of the river and marvelling at the Manx shearwaters skimming the white horses on Loch Scavaig. Sadly, any form of mountaineering was out of the question.

CHAPTER 20

Monadh Liath

GEAL CHARN (Monadh Liath) 3036ft/926m

29 December 1966 With my brothers Oliver and Christopher from Crathie near Laggan. We chose this mountain because the day did not start promising with low cloud and snow. However, as so often happens, the clouds rolled back to give us a superb day of sunshine and at times we were in shirt sleeves. At 3.30 p.m. though, when the sun disappeared, everything froze hard within minutes. We walked up Glen Markie, crossed the burn with difficulty and traversed Geal Charn from south to north. The mountain has a fine eastern corrie and there were impressive cornices and extensive views. Particularly prominent was Creag Meagaidh.

Glen Markie showed much evidence of the recent severe floods. In places the burn had altered course and huge boulders, torn from the hillside, were strewn over a wide area. On the hillside itself acres of peat and heather had been stripped off. In the gorge we could see the water level had been 15ft higher than the present level. A 5 hour day from Crathie.

CARN DEARG 3093ft/945m
CARN BAN 3087ft/942m
CARN BALLACH 3020ft/920m
CARN SGULAIN 3015ft/920m
A'CHAILLEACH (Monadh Liath) 3045ft/930m

28 October 1970 I left Glen Banchor near Newton-more at 7.30 a.m. It was a lovely red dawn with clear skies and frozen ground. The snow level was 2,000ft. I followed the good track beside the Allt Fionndrigh until it petered out and then crossed the watershed towards Carn Dearg which was snow-plastered and gleaming white in the sunshine. I climbed up the steep snow slopes almost directly under the summit. Foolishly I had left my ice-axe in the car and I had quite a lot of trouble surmounting a small cornice. While I was struggling up I lost a bar of chocolate out of my anorak pocket; this was a pity as I had lost the rest of my lunch while jumping a swollen burn. I was on Carn Dearg at 9.30 a.m. and had superb views all round, particularly towards Ben Alder and Creag Meagaidh groups.

Clouds were building up in the west so I hastened across the snowy wastes taking in Carn Ban, Carn Ballach, Carn Sgulain and finally A'Chailleach. The clouds were still just above the tops which was just as well, as in misty weather I would never have found the summit cairns. The Monadh Liath are very featureless and the summits only slight excrescences above the plateau level.

I descended down the Allt a' Chaorainn and reached the car, very hungry, at 1.10 p.m.

My second visit to the Monadh Liath arose rather unexpectedly in October 1982.

I left Ullapool early, promising myself a leisurely drive down to Northumberland with coffee and a browse round the splendid collection of books at Landmark, followed by tea and some early Christmas shopping in Edinburgh. But it was not to be.

Clear skies overnight had produced a sharp drop in temperature and the verges of the road were white with hoar frost. It had been a wet October but now, in the last week of the month, a high pressure system had moved over Scotland and I knew I could expect a glorious day. The trees beside the A9 were at their colourful autumnal best and a sprinkling of snow on Braeriach stirred emotions deep within me. I swung off the Newtonmore by-pass into the old town and stopped to buy the local Ordnance Survey map and a picnic lunch – it was only 9.30 a.m. but the sun had already broken through early mist.

It had to be the Monadh Liath, the Cairngorms' unfashionable neighbour to the west of the Spey and a range that I had last visited way back in 1970.

I drove along the narrow road leading into Glen Banchor until, after a mile, I was stopped by a locked gate bearing a notice to the effect that walkers should keep off the hills between October 9 and 21, because of deer-stalking with high-velocity rifles. It was October 25 so I was in the clear and I strode off through the bracken and heather beside the Allt a' Chaorainn making my way towards A'Chailleach which was clearly visible to the north.

After 30 minutes I crossed the burn on rounded ice-covered boulders and started climbing steeply. By chance my route passed the tiny bothy marked on the map at 687022 and I paused to peer into the dark recess of its single room. Although cladded in corrugated iron on the outside, the bothy was lined with wood and contained a few sticks of furniture and a fireplace.

The southern slopes of A'Chailleach are rounded and featureless and typical of much of the Monadh Liath. Fortunately the black peat bogs which characterise much of the high ground were frozen solid, yet my exertions and the sun's warmth allowed me to wear shirt-sleeves. I revelled in the space, the solitude and the complete freedom; my only companions being a small herd of hinds, their white rumps bobbing as they speedily made off at my approach, and a pair of ptarmigan looking plump and foolish in their premature white plumage.

Proceeding north towards Carn Sgulain I dropped down to cross a burn running through a deep defile which, having escaped the sun's rays, was chill and icy and I was glad to return to the sunshine of the tops. I paused beside the grey mica schist cairn on Carn Sgulain and looked about. I was particularly impressed by the vast expanse of wild country to the north; barren, desolate, rolling hills split only by the upper reaches of the river Findhorn. To be lost in the northern Monadh Liath on a stormy winter's night could well be fatal and I shuddered at the thought. Route-finding on today's round, however, was easy enough in such perfect conditions and, even in mist, it would pose few problems for the next three Munros, Carn Sgulain, Carn Ballach and Carn Ban are linked by the remnants of an old fence. Bits of rusty wire, half buried in the peat, kept tripping me up.

It is fast walking across the four miles of undulating wastes to Carn Ban and I was coaxed on by the steep west face of Carn Dearg, a mile south of Carn Ban, which made a prominent feature. The tiny lochan one mile north of Carn Ballach was already frozen and would, I thought, remain so until next April.

I ate a late lunch on Carn Ban, disturbing a flock of snow bunting which wheeled away, turning together and flashing in the sunshine. Below me, to the west, a huge herd of deer were grazing the moss and the stags were roaring and belling continuously. Only the massifs of Braeriach, Ben Alder and Creag Meagaidh had a dusting of snow and I thought back to the previous year's late October when I traversed the Ben Lawers range in full winter conditions.

The south summit of Carn Dearg is on a narrowish ridge – at any rate narrow by Monadh Liath standards. It afforded a good view down to the impressive Coire nan Laogh and Loch Dubh which has two streams falling in cascades over a black cliff into its dark waters.

I met no track in Glen Balloch until I reached the banks of the river Calder in Glen Banchor. But then, pacing out along a level path, I could savour the last few miles back to the car, brimming with satisfaction at five Munros achieved with ease in exquisite country. 5 hours 20 minutes for the round trip.

CHAPTER 21

Creag Meagaidh

CARN LIATH (Creag Meagaidh) 3298ft/1006m
STOB POITE COIRE ARDAIR 3460ft/1053m
CREAG MEAGAIDH 3700ft/1130m
BEINN A' CHAORAINN (Creag Meagaidh) 3437ft/1052m

20 March 1963 From Aberarder with my wife on a warm and sunny spring day. Patchy snow below 3,000ft but the cliffs of Coire Ardair and the north-facing slopes had a good covering of winter snow. We saw lizards basking on rocks in the sunshine as we ascended Carn Liath in shirt sleeves. We walked along to Stob Poite Coire Ardair, descended to the Window, the low col under Creag Meagaidh, and then traversed Creag Meagaidh and Beinn a' Chaorainn beyond. Beinn a' Chaorainn has a mile-long east face of cliffs but the summit ridge is broad and the south ridge provides a quick and simple way down to the road.

On the previous day we had ascended Creag Meagaidh by the long south ridge from Craigbeg. After reaching the summit in mist, poor compass work made us confuse Coire Ardair with Moy Corrie and by the time we had sorted ourselves out it was time to return. In April 1974 I was with a party of schoolboys ascending the mountain from Coire Ardair via the Window. The snow was hard and icy and we had to cut steps up to, and again beyond, the Window to reach the summit plateau.

[handwritten: I was in this party.]

CHAPTER 22

Ben Nevis

BEN NEVIS 4406ft/1344m
CARN MOR DEARG 4012ft/1223m

An OUMC meet at the CIC Hut. The meet was
enlivened by the presence of Robin Smith and Dougal
Haston living riotously in the hut and whooping it up on
the Ben during the day. Conditions were perfect.

24 March 1960   North-East Buttress with Jim Murray.
We reached the ridge by the Green Hollow Route and
thereafter we enjoyed a magnificent snow and ice
climb. The party ahead of us took two hours to
surmount the Mantrap but we found no particular
difficulty there. The pitch above however required two
pegs for protection. This is one of the finest
mountaineering days available in Scotland.

That week I also climbed the Ben via No. 2 Gully,
Gardyloo Gully and Tower Ridge. After climbing
Tower Ridge we walked round to Carn Mor Dearg.
The ridge leading to the Carn Mor Dearg arête was a
sheet of bare ice. This is a notoriously dangerous place
as the slopes end precipitously over Coire Leis. We
wore crampons and cut small steps. From Carn Mor
Dearg we had the best standing glissade ever, 1500ft
straight down to the CIC Hut.

In 1955 I went up and down Ben Nevis, using the
tedious track from Glen Nevis, in 2 hours 20 minutes.

CHAPTER 23

The Mamores

SGURR A' MHAIM 3601ft/1099m
AM BODACH 3382ft/1032m
STOB COIRE A' CHAIRN 3219ft/981m
NA GRUAGAICHEAN 3442ft/1055m
BINNEIN MOR 3700ft/1128m

17 March 1961 I first climbed the main peaks of the Mamores with Alan Wedgwood after we had spent several frustrating days at the CIC Hut with most of the Ben Nevis routes out of condition. We left from the road bridge over the falls in upper Glen Nevis. After a steep 3,300ft ascent up the north-west shoulder of Sgurr a' Mhaim and a traverse of the sharp Devil's Ridge (south ridge), we had a splendid day on the main ridge of the Mamores. The weather was fine and the snow conditions were excellent for walking. We were not interested in climbing Munros at that time and left a number of peaks for another day. From Binnein Mor we ran down the north-west slopes through the snow to upper reaches of Glen Nevis two miles to the west of Steall.

MULLACH NAN COIREAN 3077ft/939m
STOB BAN 3274ft/999m
AN GEARANACH 3200ft/982m

20 April 1965 With Nigel and Janet Rogers, Patrick

Duncan and Susan Grimshaw. This was a superb day's walking in the Mamores on good snow and with hot sunshine. From half-way along Glen Nevis we made our way up the north ridge eastwards to the prominent summit of Stob Ban which has several good rock faces. On Am Bodach we saw the tracks of a fox raised above the general snow level. The pressure of the fox's paws had consolidated the snow and prevented it from being blown away. The An Garbhanach – An Gearanach ridge was very narrow and exposed. We had extensive views all day from Ben Cruachan to Ben Alder.

A quick descent northwards from An Gearanach to Steall then across the suspension bridge to the Glen Nevis path. A 9-hour day at a leisurely pace.

SGURR EILDE MOR 3279ft/1008m
BINNEIN BEAG 3083ft/940m

2 October 1965 With Oliver Gilbert from Kinlochleven. We had been camping in Glencoe but the weather was wet and too bad for rock climbing so we decided to complete my ascents of the Mamores by doing the last two mountains.

We followed a good track leading to the Coire an Lochain under Sgurr Eilde Mor and as we climbed the mountain the weather improved. The rain stopped and patches of blue sky appeared although the clouds were still low over the Aonach Eagach. Oliver collected a rucksack full of lichen specimens, most of them still attached to the parent rock. We wondered if there were not herds of cattle beneath us as bellows and snorts were reaching us through the mist. However, on descending we found the Coire a' Binnein full of deer. One large herd of about forty were led by a real monarch with huge antlers and a dark brown coat. He was belling continuously while smaller herds of young stags were encircling. Other stags, also belling, had smaller herds of hinds in tow. We were witnessing the fierce competition for hinds between the old and young stags. There must have been 200 deer in the corrie.

We lunched by a delightful lochan under Binnein Beag and, on climbing the mountain, found it to be an attractive sharp little peak giving excellent views of the Mamores, Nevis and the Aonachs. We ambled down Glen Nevis in warm afternoon sunshine after a relaxing day of only a small programme of Munros.

CHAPTER 24

The Grey Corries and the Aonachs

STOB COIRE EASAIN 3658ft/1116m
STOB A' COIRE MHEADHOIN 3610ft/1106m
STOB BAN (Loch Treig) 3217ft/977m
STOB COIRE CLAURIGH 3858ft/1177m
STOB COIRE AN LAOIGH 3659ft/1115m
SGURR CHOINNICH MOR 3603ft/1095m
AONACH BEAG (Lochaber) 4060ft/1236m
AONACH MOR 3999ft/1219m

12 April 1966 After an overnight drive Oliver and I slept in the waiting room of Tyndrum Upper Station. In the morning Nigel and Janet Rogers met us and we all caught the 8.15 a.m. train to Corrour Siding. It was a bitterly cold day, the clouds were low and there was snow in the air but coffee and toast in the restaurant car cheered us up. When we disembarked at 9.45 a.m. at Corrour the sun was nearly through.

We followed the railway track north for three miles and then descended to Creaguaineach Lodge on Loch Treig side. There was a shepherd in residence in company with a shaggy horse, a foal, many dogs and a puppy.

We ascended Stob Coire Easain by its south ridge, dumping rucksacks below the summit to be picked up later. There was a very strong icy wind and much snow on both Easain and Stob a' Coire Mheadhoin which lay beyond and which we climbed also. At times we were blinded by swirling ice spicules which were driven over the corniced ridges by the wind.

It was a strange day dominated by the wind, at times the sun came through but more often it was cloudy. We picked up our rucksacks again and descended to the Lairig Leacach where we found a delightful camp site alongside the burn near a series of spectacular cascades. We were just below the snow line. Although it was only 5 p.m. we felt lethargic so established camp, leaving Stob Ban for the morrow.

Oliver and I had a Blacks Mountain Tent with flysheet but Nigel and Janet bivouacked in a nylon bag although they cooked in the tent. It was a clear and intensely cold night.

13 April 1966   It dawned fine and we were off by 8.15 a.m. and traversed Stob Ban *en route* to Stob Coire Claurigh and the Grey Corries.

The traverse of the Grey Corries was delightful. It was still cold but less windy than the previous day and the sun shone brilliantly. We had magnificent views of the Aonachs with their huge cornices, Nevis plastered white with new snow, the Mamores and many of the Argyll hills.

Sgurr Choinnich Mor with its steep sharp ridge gave us quite a sporting climb. The snow was for the most part in good condition for kicking steps which saved hours of work with the axe. At times however it was glazed with ice and later in the day we needed our crampons.

At 3.15 p.m. we had 20 minutes rest on the col below Aonach Beag and decided to press on over the Aonachs. The east ridge was extremely steep and after overcoming two pretty difficult sections we were turned back by a 20ft pitch of near vertical snow and ice just below the main ridge proper. The position was very exposed and we regarded an attempt unjustified without a rope and with our heavy packs.

However by descending 500ft and cramponing left across steep slopes Oliver led a route up a gully that had only a small cornice topping it, thus gaining access to a subsidiary ridge of Aonach Beag.

This manoeuvre cost us an hour and it was 6 p.m. when we reached the summit of Aonach Beag. We were very tired now, and it became misty, but we slowly descended the tricky ridge to the col below Aonach Mor and struggled on to this mountain's characterless top.

There was a superb sunset behind Ben Nevis as we toiled over the wastes of frozen snow until the north ridge dipped gradually down. We finally camped at 8.30 p.m. at about 1900ft, just below the snowline and near water. Once again it was a very cold night with water freezing immediately it was stilled and our boots freezing hard even in the tent.

We could see the glow of heather fires in the glen below and we ate hot reconstituted dried meat-loaf, left over from a Himalayan expedition, washed down with whisky. It had been one of the finest days I could remember having spent on the hills.

We rose next morning at 9 a.m. when the sun reached the tent and had a most delightful 1½-hour walk down the road, through forestry plantations in warm sunshine. After a relaxing day in Fort William we caught the afternoon train back to Bridge of Orchy.

CHAPTER 25

Corrour

BEINN NA LAP 3066ft/937m
CHNO DEARG 3433ft/1047m
STOB COIRE SGRIODAIN 3211ft/976m
CARN DEARG 3080ft/941m
SGOR GAIBHRE 3124ft/955m

20 April 1968 Christopher and I caught the 9.01 a.m. train from Rannoch Station to Corrour. I always enjoy this spectacular journey across Rannoch Moor with the snow tunnels, bridges and viaducts over the burns. I enjoy too the ease and comfort with which one moves across such difficult terrain.

There had been a recent mild spell and the snow level had receded to nearly 3,000ft.

From Corrour Station we took the easy west ridge up Beinn na Lap and then descended the northern slopes to the Ealaidh Glen under Chno Dearg. There was an impressive-looking rock face on the west side of the corrie facing south on Chno Dearg and we noted it for future exploration.

We needed to use the compass on the broad ridge connecting Chno Dearg with Stob Coire Sgriodain as the clouds were down but once we had located the cairn on Sgriodain, poised on the cliff-edge overlooking Loch Treig, visibility improved. The view west was dominated by the snow covered Stob a' Coire Mheadhoin and Stob Coire Easain but the Grey

Corries were in cloud. We could see across Loch Laggan to the Creag Meagaidh group and to the east the Aonach Beag ridge and Beinn a' Chlachair.

We descended the north ridge and followed the railway line to Tulloch Station. The sun came out and we had a pleasant 45-minute wait for the 5 p.m. train back to Corrour. We just had time to locate the buffet car for a quick tea before being deposited once more at the lonely station of Corrour.

We collected our packs from the Waiting Room and carried them up to a camp site at about 2,000ft on the slopes of Carn Dearg.

21 April 1968   The night was dry which was lucky for we were bivouacking under a tent flysheet. It was a grey morning and we were off at 8.00 a.m. to the summit of Carn Dearg. Beyond, at the col marked Mam Ban, we dumped our rucksacks and raced up and down Sgor Gaibhre.

The route back to Rannoch Station lay six miles down the very peat-hag ridden Glen Eigheach. We found the going was easiest near the burn and further down the glen it was picturesque with gorges, cascades and falls. The sun came out and we wore shirt sleeves for the last few miles. We reached Rannoch Station at 1 p.m.

CHAPTER 26

Ben Alder Forest

BEINN A' CHLACHAIR 3569ft/1088m
CREAG PITRIDH 3031ft/924m
GEAL CHARN (Ben Alder Forest) 3443ft/1049m

30 May 1963 At the start of a very hot spell of weather Trisha and I drove down the rough road alongside Loch Ericht, passed Benalder Lodge and left the car near Loch Pattack. We camped beside the Allt Cam and had to immerse the butter in the burn to stop it melting.

In the afternoon we ascended Beinn a' Chlachair by the broad east ridge. There were still patches of old snow and the summit was a superb viewpoint for the Nevis range, the Grey Corries and Creag Meagaidh. There is an attractive north-facing corrie ringed with cliffs.

We could look down to the pimple of Creag Pitridh which looks far too insignificant to be a Munro but makes the necessary height by thirty-one feet. We descended easily to the col above Loch Leamhain and then walked over Creag Pitridh and Geal Charn and so back to our camp. A delightful walk that took 4½ hours.

In April 1974 I returned to this area with Rob Musker and some boys from Ampleforth College. We walked from the west end of Loch Laggan up the good

stalking track towards the Beinn a' Chlachair – Geal
Charn col. There was moor burning going on and it was
beautifully warm. We camped at 2,400ft beside the
stream and in the afternoon walked up Beinn a'
Chlachair. The corrie and upper slopes were filled with
snow and we skirted the edge of Coire Mor. The boys
were able to glissade down the slopes to the camp by
sitting on their cagoules. We cooked supper over a
heather and bogwood fire.

The following day was sunny and hot and we walked
up Geal Charn without shirts on. As on Beinn a'
Chlachair there was a large well-constructed cairn.
While glissading down steep slopes towards Creag
Pitridh one of the boys skinned the back of his hands on
the hard crystalline snow – he was not wearing gloves!
This was one of the best periods of spring weather ever
recorded in the Highlands. For six weeks a high
pressure system was stationary over central Scotland
and gave perfect sunny and dry weather, hot during the
day and frosty at night. I was lucky enough to be able to
enjoy two weeks of this weather. The hillsides were dry
as a bone and one could have a whole day out with dry
feet. Over in the west we swam at Gruinard Bay in
summer weather.

BHEINN BHEOIL 3333ft/1019m
BEN ALDER 3757ft/1148m
CARN DEARG 3391ft/1034m
GEAL CHARN (Ben Alder Forest) 3688ft/1132m
AONACH BEAG (Ben Alder Forest) 3646ft/1114m
BEINN EIBHINN 3611ft/1100m

31 May 1963 The day dawned fine and it soon
became baking hot. The mountains were shimmering in
heat haze with not a cloud in sight. We walked up a

good stalking track to Loch a' Bhealaich Bheithe and then completed the Bheinn Bheoil – Ben Alder horseshoe. The Ben Alder cliffs were still ringed with snow and the summit plateau held a large snowfield. We descended the narrow and exciting north-east ridge to the glen. The burns were brimming with melted snow water and we plunged into a deep pool to cool off.

1 June 1963   The next day was even hotter and we had to protect our skin from the sun. We climbed the ridge behind our tent on to Carn Dearg, then we had a delightful undulating walk over Geal Charn, Aonach Beag and Beinn Eibhinn. We reached the summit of the latter, our fourth Munro, after 4 hours and we had lunch. We could see a train puffing across Rannoch Moor away to the west. Aonach Beag is a particularly shapely mountain with a steep triangular-shaped face on the north side.

Returning to the col under Beinn Eibhinn we descended to the north reaching the glen under Beinn a' Chlachair. Again today we saw many herds of deer and ptarmigan that had mostly lost their winter plumage. From the glen it was an extremely hot six mile walk back to camp.

When we arrived back we immersed ourselves for a long time in the burn. Indeed we sat reading with the water up to our waists and our heads shrouded. There was no shade and the tent was like an oven.

In November 1974, together with Paul Hawksworth and Gerard Simpson, I returned to the Ben Alder area, walking in from the west. We carried supplies for three days and a lightweight tent to be used only in emergencies as we intended to stay in bothies.

We left Rannoch Station at 10.30 a.m. on a morning of low cloud and drizzle. At first we walked for a mile up the railway track but then we crossed saturated hillsides, going east past Lochan Sron Smeur and Lochan Loin nan Donnlaich. This area is remote so we were surprised to see a new access road bulldozed across the hillsides and a large area enclosed and drained ready for afforestation.

By Loch Ericht side we met a good track. In spite of incessant rain we could appreciate the beauty of the area with stands of Caledonian pine and larch. We saw an eagle and many herds of deer. Below the clouds all we could see were mountainsides streaked with snow. At 3 p.m. we reached Alder Bay and Benalder Cottage. It was a delightful spot and the cottage was solid, made of stone, and had three rooms. The Alder burn had to be crossed to reach the cottage and luckily a makeshift log bridge had been erected by the Mountain Bothies Association. It would have been unfordable otherwise. We collected wood for a fire and dried out slowly during the evening keeping a look out for the ghost of the stalker McCook. At that time it was believed that McCook, years ago, had hanged himself from a beam in the passage. The story is now known to be false but the eerie image of the cottage remains.

After an uneventful night the morning dawned clear and cold. We set off up to Bealach Breabag where we dumped our packs and walked over Sron Coire na h'Iolaire to Bheinn Bheoil. We had distant views of the Cairgorms shining white with fresh snow in the sunshine. Collecting our packs again we walked up the other side of the horseshoe to the Ben Alder plateau. Winter had arrived here, the freezing level was about 1,500ft and the plateau was snow covered and the cliffs already corniced. It was too cold to linger on the summit so we climbed with care down the verglassed rocks of the narrow north-east ridge. An excellent stalkers' track led us to Culra Lodge bothy where we spent the night. This is another solid and comfortable bothy with box bunks. We had it to ourselves apart from the rats and mice whose droppings were everywhere. As a precaution we suspended our food in rucksacks from hooks in the beams. The skies cleared and we enjoyed a wonderful sunset over Ben Alder as a hard frost descended.

We were off at 9 a.m. next morning toiling up the slopes behind the bothy to Carn Dearg. We continued along the ridge on compass bearing in thin mist to Geal Charn and beyond to Aonach Beag and Beinn Eibhinn. The ridges were mixed rock and snow with the north-facing corries packed with fresh snow. We only had occasional glimpses east to Ben Alder and Loch Ericht. We descended 500ft westwards from the summit of Beinn Eibhinn and stopped for lunch. We saw a flock of about twenty snow buntings and many large herds of deer, the stags roaring. Our aim was to catch the 5.19 p.m. train from Corrour to Rannoch Station and we made it with 30 minutes to spare. It was a long walk down the glen to Corrour Lodge and then through sweet-smelling larch woods alongside Loch Ossian. The sun came out at last and we saw many herons on the loch. It was a perfect end to a most successful three-day walk and, perhaps because it was my second visit to this group of Munros, I enjoyed them all the more.

April 1981 was unusually fine and Gerard Simpson and I took advantage of the settled spell to revisit Ben Alder. This isolated mountain in the Central Highlands always makes an eventful and challenging expedition.

We parked the car at Bridge of Orchy station and caught the early morning train to Rannoch. This links with the post-bus which took us on to Bridge of Gaur. The track to Loch Ericht starts through the trees and then emerges onto high open moorland with the Ben Alder massif rising hugely and filling the view ahead to the north.

Lunch in the spring sunshine amongst the Caledonian pines on Loch Erichtside, and soon after we arrived at Benalder Cottage which was quite deserted. Following the recent dry spell the Alder burn was easily forded.

Recent research by Hamish Brown has shown that the stalker McCook died in his bed and reported hauntings from the cottage by Sir Robert Grieve and others must originate elsewhere. On such a sparkling afternoon we cast such thoughts aside and spent our time gathering wood and investigating Cluny's Cage which we found on the hillside after a short search.

The next morning an icy wind met us on the plateau of Ben Alder which was still very much in the grip of winter. Once down beside the Uisge Labhair, however, the sun was warm and Loch Ossian was looking as entrancing as ever.

In good conditions the ascent of Ben Alder from the cottage makes an easy day and we had time in hand before the evening train from Fort William picked us up at Corrour and whisked us back to the car at Bridge of Orchy.

CHAPTER 27

The Cairngorms

GEAL CHARN (Glen Feshie) 3019ft/920m
SGOR GAOITH 3658ft/1118m
CARN BAN MOR 3443ft/1052m
MEALL DUBHAG 3268ft/998m
MULLACH CLACH A' BHLAIR 3338ft/1019m
MONADH MOR 3651ft/1113m
CAIRN TOUL 4241ft/1291m
THE DEVIL'S POINT 3303ft/1004m
CARN A' MHAIM 3400ft/1037m
BEINN A' BHUIRD 3924ft/1196m
BEN AVON 3843ft/1171m

12 July 1969 Christopher and I left Feshie Bridge carrying light rucksacks that contained only bivouac gear and food for three days. The lower section of Glen Feshie is open and the river has a huge boulder-strewn flood plain. We climbed steeply up a hillside through a stand of Caledonian pine trees. Above 2,000ft we were enclosed in wet clinging cloud necessitating the wearing of anoraks. Geal Charn was our first summit and from there we needed to use the compass to reach the edge of the Sgoran Dubh cliffs and to locate the small cairn on Sgor Gaoith. Unfortunately we had no view of Loch Einich 2,000ft below. I found a complete but cold ptarmigan's egg lying on a small shelf of granite sand on the Gleann Einich side, this I left on the Sgor Gaoith cairn.

After Gaoith we proceeded by compass-bearing

again but when we passed a ruined bothy by a small lochan we questioned our route-finding. The hillsides were quite featureless. However we made Carn Ban Mor and passed the true bothy, marked on the O.S. map beyond. On Meall Dubhag the clouds rolled away enough for us to see down to the Feshie and glimpse the deep Coire Garbhlach below to the south.

We traversed the head of Coire Garbhlach which was truly splendid with steep cliffs and a spectacular waterfall. The wind was blowing the spray right back over the cliffs and we rested for lunch and a pipe in a sheltered hollow.

To our surprise we crossed a rough track plus Land Rover on the open hillside of Mullach Clach a' Bhlair. The track had been recently bulldozed and was a sorry scar on the landscape. Thereafter we had a tedious 2-hour walk on a bearing across what must be one of the largest high areas of bog and peat-hag anywhere in Scotland.

It was 5 p.m. before we descended to the beautiful upper reaches of Glen Eidart with a big burn running and a few patches of blue sky overhead. The cliffs of Coire Mharconaich towered over us to the west. The next few hours over Monadh Mor were rather tedious as we were tired and the mountain has little to recommend it except for its huge bulk. At 8 p.m. we found a sheltered spot in upper Glen Geusachan for supper and bivy. We cooked an excellent meal and had good views towards the Devil's Point and Carn a' Mhaim. Even at 10.30 p.m. it was light and warm enough to sit out in comfort and the breeze kept the midges away.

We slept wrapped in groundsheets but it drizzled during the night and I was kept awake by water dripping on to my face. By breakfast time the clouds were higher and we were off again cheerfully soon after 9 a.m.

13 July 1969 A steep ascent of boiler-plate slabs took us to the col between the Devil's Point and Cairn Toul and another hour on a bearing saw us at the cairn of the latter peak. Again wet cloud obscured all view but on regaining the col and the Devil's Point we broke out of the mist and could see Corrour Bothy below and parties of walkers strung out along the Lairig Ghru.

We had some difficulty descending a steep gully off the Devil's Point which was choked with old snow and this enforced a horribly loose traverse to an easier way down. We lunched in sunshine beside the Dee.

The previous December I had made an attempt to reach the summit of Carn a' Mhaim to the east of Corrour Bothy. We had camped at Linn of Dee for the weekend and, in atrocious weather of thick mist and torrential rain, had searched the summit for the cairn. We were not convinced that we had found the true summit before we beat a retreat to the fleshpots of Braemar. The weather had been equally bad on the Sunday and since everything we had was thoroughly soaked we drove home. That was the only weekend that I have spent when I have not achieved even a single summit.

This particular day however was improving all the time. We left our sacks by the path and made a quick ascent of Carn a' Mhaim. The highest point was indeed some way north of the cairn we had reached previously. We walked on past Derry Lodge and took the small path from Glen Lui to Glen Quoich. It was a delightful area of cliffs and lochans; I saw an adder curled up on the peat and we surprised a clutch of young grouse with

10 Our New Year camp in 1968 in Coire Etchachan. Christopher Gilbert checks the tent in preparation to withstand another night of violent storms.

11   Nigel and Janet Rogers and I setting off up the slopes of Stob Ban
on the second day of our traverse of the Grey Corries from
Corrour to Fort William (Easter 1966).

12   On the summit of Beinn a'Bhuird after a three-day traverse
of the Cairngorms in July 1969.

13   Members of my Ampleforth College party in Glen Einich (Cairngorms)
on a sparkling morning in 1979. It is well to remember that a carefree
scene such as this belies the underlying seriousness of expeditions
with young people to remote areas in winter. Good training,
planning and equipment are essential.

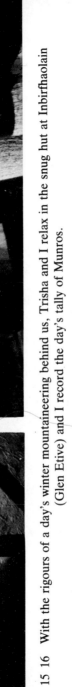

Ben Cruachan group above Loch Awe (left horizon). *Photo: Bert Jenkins*

15 16 With the rigours of a day's winter mountaineering behind us, Trisha and I relax in the snug hut at Inbirfhaolain (Glen Etive) and I record the day's tally of Munros.

17 A view from Sron na Creise (Black Mount), past Buachaille Etive Mor, to Ben Nevis and the Lochaber peaks.

18 A high-pressure system over the Cairngorms can give exhilarating weather in early spring. Here, my Ampleforth College colleagues Gerard Simpson and Basil Postlethwaite strike up the west shoulder of Breariach

19   Caution thrown to the winds in a spontaneous action of elation on the verglassed O.S. Pillar of Ben Alder after my third ascent of this remote and legendary peak in 1981.

the mother putting on a most convincing lame-wing act. Glen Quoich too looked charming in the evening sunshine with its good stands of Caledonian pine, but new forestry tracks spoiled much of the view. A golden eagle soared over us for a time until its curiosity was satisfied. Soon after Quoich Water turned east all traces of the path disappeared and we had a tiring hour bashing through deep heather and pine trees before we broke out on to the open hillside above. At 9 p.m. we found a delectable bivvy site at 2,000ft beside the Allt-an-t-Sneachda. A rough wall marked the site of an ancient enclosure and we made ourselves snug using this as a wind break and the groundsheet as awning. The sun was out on Carn Elrig Mor opposite us and we were right up to schedule, being well placed for Beinn a' Bhuird the next day.

14 July 1969   The sun woke us at 6 a.m. and we were off early but there was still mist hanging round the tops. Route-finding was easy by keeping to the cliff edges of Coire na Ciche and Coire na Clach. At 9 a.m. the sun broke right through and we reached the summit of Beinn a' Bhuird, a fine mountain with steep corries to the east and north. The plateau was covered with lumps of quartz and we searched for Cairngorm stones but found instead a family of young ptarmigan.

We paused for a second breakfast at the Sneck, the low col between Beinn a' Bhuird and Ben Avon and could see some way into the Garbh Coire; we identified the Mitre Ridge. The sun shone strongly but the breeze on the tops made it a very pleasant day. A helicopter appeared overhead. We thought it either could be going to Balmoral or could be plotting the whereabouts of the deer before the start of the stalking season. The summit of Ben Avon is a high granite tor and we basked in the sunshine eating oranges and enjoying a tremendous view to the north. It was 11 a.m.

Not using the compass I made an unfortunate error of route-finding on our descent to Inchrory Lodge. This necessitated a long descent through heather and hags down the Feith Laoigh. The burn itself was a delight and we could see trout darting as our shadows passed over the water. Just before Inchrory we immersed ourselves in the burn as it was scorchingly hot. Inchrory is a well kept lodge and the river Avon flowing beside it is a large river and a fisherman's paradise. We took the six-mile track past Delnadamph Lodge to Cock Bridge where we arrived at 5 p.m. We hitched from there back to the car at Feshie Bridge without too much trouble.

The Cairngorms lend themselves to backpacking expeditions at any time of the year. Exhilarating conditions can be encountered in March, but you should be prepared for wintry weather as the following account shows:

25 March 1976 We are camped in the glen of the Eidart, by the confluence with the Caochan Dubh. Deep snow everywhere and we cleared a platform for Paul's mountain tent. All around is a very wintry scene indeed; the corries corniced, avalanche debris under the steep slopes and the burns covered over with snow. The wind is icy and flurries of snow are sweeping down the glen, but we are snug and very well fed and brewed.

We started this morning from Lagganlia in Glen Feshie at 9.15 a.m., Paul, myself and six boys. Fortunately we were able to find a path up through the Caledonian pines which led us to the upper slopes of Geal Charn. Nick was soon in trouble, gasping and exhausted, so we divided up much of his gear amongst us. This improved matters but all day he was tired and lagging behind. Admittedly we had heavy loads; food, tents and winter equipment for six day's backpacking.

The previous few weeks in the Cairngorms had been exceptionally severe with deep snow, blizzards and avalanches causing several deaths. The lower, south-facing slopes were surprisingly free of snow but once near Sgor Gaoith all was changed. It was misty and we had showers of snow all day, limiting views of the heavily-corniced Sgoran Dubh cliffs.

The plateau over to Carn Ban Mor and Meall Dubhag was bleak and snowy and we had a long detour round the deep chasm of Coire Garbhlach which looked most impressive in the mists. Thereafter the snow conditions became much worse, deep and corniced even over the banks of small burns.

The slopes leading up to Mullach Clach a'Bhlair had recently avalanched, so we left them for another occasion and proceeded on compass bearing towards the Eidart. Following the Caochan Dubh burn, although snowed over, was all right at first but later we ran into steep, rocky ground and things became decidedly dicy. The boys were slithering and falling about so I changed tactics and crossed the burn, traversed the hill on the north-east side and then managed to find a reasonable descent to the Eidart from the north. It was past 5 p.m. and snowing hard and we could have been in trouble if we had continued to force our way down the burn.

Now we are safe and snug, although the wind and snow are buffeting the tent. I think we are all satisfied with four Munros in such conditions with heavy packs. Across the Eidart rise the steep flanks of Monadh Mor which we may tackle tomorrow. There was nothing on

the hills today except ptarmigan, sensibly the deer have
retreated to lower ground.

26 March   About an inch of fresh snow fell overnight
and the day's work started with 800ft of step kicking up
the slopes beyond the river to reach the plateau of
Monadh Mor. The weather deteriorated with a tearing
wind and snow storms on and off all day. Visibility was
poor and, after reaching the cairn, we dropped down as
quickly as possible to the head of Glen Geusachan. It
was not the day to spend long on the tops, and once
again I was worried by Nick, who was very slow and
permanently cold as he couldn't seem to manage his
equipment. He lost his gloves and was unable to cope
with his anorak hood. We lunched beside the snowed-
over river while the flakes swirled round, and then
spent the afternoon negotiating the rough glen. It took
hours of stumbling over buried rocks and heather and
through covered pools before we finally made Corrour
Bothy at 4.15 p.m.

The bothy was wet and filthy. The earth floor had a
few pieces of muddy polythene sheet as covering and
Paul and I preferred to camp outside.

27 March   A wild night with great buffets of wind
roaring down the glen and hitting the tent. In the early
hours the snow turned to lashing rain and the gale
increased. The ridge pole bent into a bow and several
guy ropes broke but we remained dry. For not the first
time we were thankful that we had decided to carry the
extra weight of a tough, well-proven tent. A lightweight
nylon tent could hardly have survived. The bad weather
continued all day and we read and dozed. Two men
arrived, plastered in snow, from the Sinclair Memorial
Hut, the crossing having taken 7 hours.

28 March   The rain stopped and the tent quickly dried

in the strong wind. As we walked up the Lairig Ghru a break appeared in the clouds and we decided to try for Ben Macdui and then descend to Coire Etchachan. Leaving the path we struggled upwards over steep slopes of snow-covered rocks against a monumental wind. The gusts were fantastic and felled us like ninepins. Patrick was lifted bodily up, pack and all, and dashed on the rocks fully five yards away. When we were about 800ft from the top of Macdui it was agreed that we must retreat. There would have been risk of injury on the Cairngorm plateau. The wind was probably equal to that which Christopher and I experienced on Derry Cairngorm in January 1968, during the gale which caused structural damage throughout Scotland.

Back in the Lairig we found the path very tiresome with a deep covering of wet snow, but it was cheering to catch the occasional glimpse of sunshine on the vast cornices of Braeriach. At last we found a sheltered camp site beside the burn at the bottom of a shallow ravine, 500ft below the Sinclair Hut and at the upper tree-line of Rothiemurchus Forest.

A Cairngorm winter can be long and in 1976 April came with no visible sign that spring was approaching.

The round of Beinn a'Bhuird and Ben Avon makes a fine day's walk and I was able to achieve this during an exceptional spell of spring weather in April 1978.

We left our Glen Derry camp site and took the connecting path between glens Lui and Quoich. Glen Quoich is a wonderful sight early on a sunny morning, with its swift, sparkling river, stands of Scots pine and, as background, the vast bulks of Beinn a'Bhuird and Ben Avon rising snow-clad into a blue sky. The pines

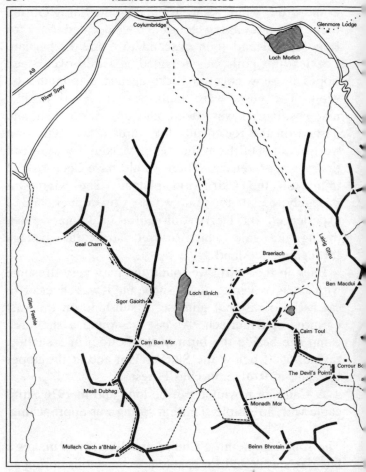

smelled sweet, the burns were brimming with melt water and the sun was hot. This was Scotland at its best.

To reach the north side of Quoich Water it was necessary to wade a large tributary burn, but thereafter easy heathery slopes led up Bruach Mhor at the south end of the Beinn a'Bhuird ridge. Once on the plateau we kept well away from the cliff-edge because the huge

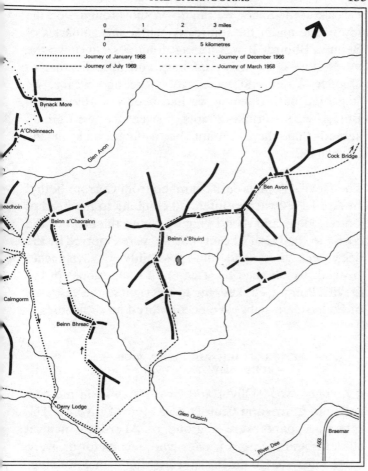

cornices were cracking and creaking ominously.

The Sneck was just clear of snow and we left our rucksacks in a pile and made a lightning ascent and descent of Ben Avon, in 50 minutes. This included a memorable five minutes spent sitting in the sun on the granite tor of Ben Avon admiring the magnificent sweep of the Garbh Coire.

Back at the Sneck we ran down snow tongues on the south side under the impressive cliffs and pinnacles of Beinn a'Bhuird. It was a long, long descent down the lower slopes, through peat hags and deep heather to Quoich Water and when, foot-sore and weary, we staggered back to camp we had been out 10½ hours. But, as we sat drinking pints of sweet tea, we were all agreed that there cannot be a finer walk in the Highlands.

The Devil's Point is easily climbed from Corrour bothy. In April 1982 we had intended climbing to the head of Coire Odhar and then swinging round the head of the corrie to the Devil's Point, but we were deterred by the deep wet snow and the possibility of avalanche. Instead, we climbed the steep and rocky slopes of the Devil's Point itself, keeping to the right of the vast area of boiler-plate slabs. We encountered no difficulties.

CARN CLOICH-MHUILLINN 3087ft/942m
BEINN BHROTAIN 3795ft/1157m

6 January 1965   Oliver and I were staying at the new splendid Cairngorm Club Hut at Muir of Inverey. The other occupants were a group of Aberdeen medical students and their girl friends who, luckily for us, were more interested in the fire and cooking than in walking. In view of the snow conditions they were sensible. They cooked for us and fed us on home made oatcakes and haggis.

Following recent heavy snowfalls a thaw had set in and the Linn of Dee was roaring with melt-water. We walked along the good track to White Bridge at the junction of the Dee and the Geldie burn. Some stalkers out culling hinds had driven their Land Rover into bog up to its axles; they were bad tempered and they lectured us on the foolhardiness of making for the high tops in such conditions. The week before there had been a fatal accident on Beinn a' Bhuird.

At White Bridge we kept to the Dee and, after a mile or so, struck up into the mist on compass bearing on to the east flank of the featureless bulk of Carn Cloich-mhuillinn. Soon after 1 p.m. we reached the bleak small cairn and, huddling together out of the wind, ate our lunch of cold pork chops and cold roast potatoes. Not a good choice in the circumstances. We slogged on for another 1½ hours to reach Beinn Bhrotain but time did not allow us to continue to Monadh Mor. It was a tedious 4-hour walk back to Inverey, the last 2 hours being in darkness.

BEINN BHREAC 3051ft/931m
BEINN A' CHAORAINN (Cairngorms) 3553ft/1082m
BEINN MHEADHOIN 3883ft/1182m
DERRY CAIRNGORM 3788ft/1155m

12 January 1968 After a snowy all-night drive up from the south and quite a bit of trouble on the Devil's Elbow, Christopher and I left Linn of Dee at 9 a.m. It was a cold and clear day with deep snow everywhere and Glen Derry was full of deer brought down by the recent bad weather. We were carrying a tent and provisions for four days. Before reaching Derry Lodge we left the path and made our way up the slopes of Meall an Lundain. The conditions were bad for walking as one foot would hold on the snow crust and the next would go in calf deep. This went on all day and being unfit I found it quite exhausting. Beyond Beinn Bhreac, above a small ravine, we found a rain gauge sticking up out of the snow with a two-foot deep collecting tank. After lunch the sun came out and the Cairngorms plastered in snow looked at their best.

We continued painstakingly across the featureless plateau to the summit of Beinn a' Chaorainn, three miles to the north of Beinn Bhreac, and then ploughed down the western slopes to Coire Etchachan and made camp at 4 p.m. It was extremely cold and although the burn was running under the snow, still water froze in the billy almost immediately. The eggs had to be prized out of their shells. However, we tied up the sleeve entrance of the tent and made ourselves snug with the stove, supper and a bottle of whisky.

13 January 1968   During the night it snowed and in the morning the clouds were right down to the tent. We ambled up to the Etchachan Hut which was hard to find with the visibility only forty yards. The hut was extremely cold and squalid and we were glad we had our tent.

At 12 noon we decided to have a go at Beinn Mheadhoin and left on a compass bearing up steep snow and rocks. At the 3,500ft level we broke out above the clouds with glorious views and patches of blue sky above. The cairn was perched on a vast 20ft boulder and we scrambled up over deep frost feathers. Of course the high wind had obliterated our footprints so we had to recourse to the compass again. At times there was a white-out with visibility virtually nil and we were lucky to see a cornice and cliffs just ahead. Skirting these we descended directly to the tent. Later we ate a huge supper and finished off the whisky while the wind rose and it started to snow again.

14 January 1968   The next day the wind had torn gaps in the clouds and we struck straight up through a line of cliffs on to Derry Cairngorm. We had to do some rock scrambling and cut some steps. The last few hundred feet on to the cone-shaped summit were a real fight against the wind which was hurricane force at times and we literally had to crawl, clinging to rocks whenever possible. The sky was steely grey and threatening. We made all possible speed down the north-eastern shoulder thus avoiding the steepest cliffs and immediately packed up camp.

The 4½-mile walk to Derry Lodge was tedious and exhausting. The soft snow let us in every step going through Derry Forest and it was often knee deep. Beyond Derry Lodge the road had been snow ploughed so we made better time.

That night we slept in the car parked just off the road by the Glen Callater turn-off. It was a wild night with the wind howling and the car rocking on its springs. Returning home the following day we passed thousands of trees snapped off or torn out of the ground. We learned that 18 people had been killed by the storms in Glasgow and that a gust of 136 m.p.h. had been recorded.

Beinns Bhreac, Chaorainn and Mheadhoin can be combined in an 8-hour day from Derry Lodge. I did this walk on a wintry day in April 1978, following the Glen Derry path as far as the footbridge at ref. 039957, and then climbing straight up to the summit of Beinn Bhreac.

Compass work brought us across the barren wastes to Beinn Chaorainn and then we ran down a snow tongue for lunch beside the burn, a tributary of the River Avon. A flock of geese flew over in a typical V formation and we rescued two half frozen lizards from a snow patch, but otherwise this wintry glen appeared to be devoid of life.

After lunch we tackled the long eastern slopes of Beinn Mheadhoin (3883 ft) and visited three false granite tor summits before arriving at the true, cairned, one. Climbing the iced rocks to surmount the tor proved to be quite tricky and almost beyond the powers of one member of the party who had no rock-climbing experience.

CAIRNGORM 4084ft/1245m

18 March 1958 One of the big four of the main Cairngorm range along with Ben Macdui, Braeriach and Cairn Toul. Sadly it is now festooned with ski-tows, chair-lifts and cafes; a road has been bulldozed up the northern flanks from Loch Morlich to a height of 2,000ft.

My first ascent was years ago before any development started. Whilst on a skiing course run by the army during National Service I escaped from Aviemore for a day to walk up alone. I had little or no equipment but I walked along the top of the corniced cliffs above Coire an Lochain and enjoyed the solitude, the sunshine and the complete contrast from army life. I saw ptarmigan for the first time.

BRAERIACH 4248ft/1296m

21 March 1958 Another lone expedition from Aviemore whilst on the same skiing course. Trudging up through the Rothiemurchus Forest carrying skis and wearing ill-fitting boots was no fun at all. The descent on skis was no better for a novice and usually ended up floundering in deep snow, rocks or against a tree trunk.

On a cold clear day I walked through Glen Einich passing herds of deer and the frozen loch. Up the steep west shoulder of Braeriach to the summit plateau and the cairn. Then I traversed the top of the Garbh Coire making for Cairn Toul but on the Angel's Peak time ran out and I had to return. Although I had no ice-axe or crampons I was able to climb down into the Garbh Coire by facing in towards the slope and kicking steps. It was dicy but in those early days I didn't realise the risks I was taking. Down in the Lairig Ghru the snow was deep and it was a struggle to climb up to the top of the pass at the Pools of Dee. I met a party of grim-faced balaclavared climbers bound for Derry Lodge who had a lot to say about my lack of an axe and the foolishness of solo-climbing in winter. I agree with them about their former, but certainly not their latter point. I missed the path in the gathering darkness and floundered through trees and into snowed over burns before making Coylumbridge and finally Aviemore after over 12 hours.

Twenty-one years later, somewhat wiser, more experienced and better equipped, I made a far more satisfactory ascent of Braeriach. It was 2 April 1979, a day of keen frost and unbroken sunshine.

From Whitewell we walked up Glen Einich, our boots splintering the frozen puddles, and then cramponed up hard, crystalline snow on the shoulder of Braeriach, keeping to the right of Coire Bogha-cloiche.

Braeriach summit was arctic with massive cornices over the corries but the view was extensive and unforgettable. We returned over Sron na Lairig to the Sinclair Hut in the Lairig Ghru. A leisurely stroll through Rothiemurchus in the late afternoon sunshine brought us back to Whitewell after a 9 hour trip.

BEN MACDUI 4300ft/1309m

21 December 1962   On the shortest day of the year, but in brilliant sunshine and deep snow, Trisha and I walked over Cairngorm summit and across the high plateau to Ben Macdui. Luckily we made good time and did not linger as mist came down on our return and our thoughts turned to the Great Grey Man. We inspected Coire Cas but decided that it was too icy to descend without much step cutting so we reclimbed Cairngorm and retraced our footsteps down to Loch Morlich.

I did not return to Ben Macdui until April 1978.

We camped at an idyllic site in Glen Derry beside the river, about half a mile up-stream from Derry Lodge. A soft bed of heather for the tents and log fires every night, built safely on the gravel beside the burn, provided our every need.

After a clear and frosty night the sun rose early and we made our way through the scattered pines to the south ridge of Derry Cairngorm. By the time we reached the summit of Derry Cairngorm (2 hours) the sun was hot, the views captivating and extensive and water was in great demand; but water bottles were soon drained and mouthfuls of snow had to suffice.

We skirted Coire Sputan Dearg to the north to reach the final snow dome of Ben Macdui. The summit was crowded with skiers who had come over from Cairngorm, so we did not linger but ploughed down through sugary snow to Loch Etchachan. Although the loch was frozen we found a hole in the snow near the exit stream for long draughts of icy water.
water.

Down then to the Hutchinson Memorial Hut, which was as squalid and filthy as ever, from where we watched an avalanche pouring over the cliffs behind the hut. Still in hot sun we wearily made our way back down into Glen Derry and the track to camp. A 6 hour 50 minute day.

From Derry Lodge a far easier day's walk is up the glen to Coire Etchachan with a return over the summit of Derry Cairngorm. From Derry Cairngorm an easy ridge leads south for two miles, whence a steep but straightforward descent to Glen Derry can be made.

In early April 1982, whilst on a training camp for Arctic Norway, I did this round in 5½ hours with an Ampleforth School party, in spite of many delays caused by trouble with the boys' crampon fastenings.

A'CHOINNEACH 3345ft/1017m
BYNACK MORE 3574ft/1090m

28 December 1966 Oliver, Christopher and I walked up Cairngorm via the popular ski run, the White Lady Corrie. The snow was good but there were no skiers about due to the high wind and the early hour. The plateau was in mist so we cancelled plans for Ben Macdui and descended to the col at the north end of Loch Avon. From here we traversed A'Choinneach and Bynack More. The wind was blowing powder-snow with great force and at times we had to bury our ice-axes in the snow and hang on. We saw a white hare and there were many herds of deer in Strath Nethy. A delightful walk back to Glenmore in the afternoon sunshine.

CHAPTER 28

Drumochter

GEAL CHARN (Loch Ericht) 3005ft/917m
A'MHARCONAICH 3185ft/975m
BEINN UDLAMAIN 3306ft/1010m
SGAIRNEACH MHOR 3210ft/991m

2 June 1963 As a base to climb this group of four Munros Trisha and I camped near Balsporran Cottages in the Drumochter Pass. We had just had three excellent days in the remote Ben Alder region and we found these mountains rather unattractive. The weather was hot and we discovered no water on the ridges and we were hardly ever away from the roar of the traffic along the A9.

These are broad-ridged rounded mountains and although there is a fine high corrie on Sgairneach Mhor they would have been better left for winter conditions. We visited all the summits in a leisurely 6½-hour walk over the tops from Balsporran Cottages to Dalnaspidal Station. Although it was hot and still, mercifully there were no midges.

A'BHUIDHEANACH BHEAG 3064ft/936m
CARN NA CAIM 3087ft/941m
MEALL CHUAICH 3120ft/951m

10 July 1968 I was at Leith Docks, dropping off stores for an expedition to Iceland, on a perfect summer's

144

day. Taking advantage of this I drove north after lunch and arrived at Dalnaspidal Station at 4.30 p.m. Unfortunately the weather did not hold and in steady rain I walked up the heather covered slopes of A'Bhuidheanach Bheag. The summit was capped by a trig point and a large quartz cairn. Three miles further on over peat hags and on a compass bearing I reached Carn na Caim at 6.30 p.m. There were patches of old snow in the north-facing corries and a heavy shower of freezing rain left me shivering.

I continued a further six miles north to Meall Chuaich while the weather improved. To the east I had views down to the Lochs Bhrodainn and Seilich and to Gaick Lodge. In a bog I found a soldiers's helmet, first world war type, and carried it to Meall Chuaich where I placed it on the cairn. I also found, pathetically, some antlers attached to a skull which were tightly entangled in some old fence wire tied to an iron stake.

I ran down to Loch Cuaich and took the good track beside the aqueduct to Dalwhinnie which I reached at 10.15 p.m.

CHAPTER 29

Glen Tilt

CARN A' CHLAMAIN 3159ft/963m
CARN LIATH 3193ft/975m
BRAIGH COIRE CHRUINN-BHALGAIN 3505ft/1070m
CARN NAN GABHAR (BEINN A' GHLO) 3671ft/1129m

28 March 1964 With Oliver, Christopher, and Nigel
and Janet Rogers. We camped beside the river in Glen
Tilt just beyond Forest Lodge. The first day was so wet
and cold that we did not venture out from our tents
until 4 p.m. Then we made a quick ascent of Carn a'
Chlamain just above our camp on the north-west side of
the glen. The snow was compact and the climb was
easy, although the visibility was poor we found the
summit trig point just by following the contours up to
the highest point.

29 March 1964 The next day was much better with
clear patches of sky and the clouds were above the tops.
We walked down to Marble Lodge and climbed the
long ridge of the Beinn a' Ghlo massif consisting of the
three Munros – Carn Liath, Braigh Coire Chruinn-
bhalgain and Carn nan Gabhar. There was deep crisp
snow everywhere and at one point we saw a herd of
seventy deer, led by a stag, walking single file through
the snow across the skyline. Carn nan Gabhar was my
hundredth Munro and we enjoyed a quarter bottle of
Vat 69 on the summit. We were able to glissade much
of the way down into Glen Tilt again.

AN SGARSOCH 3300ft/1006m
CARN AN FHIDLEIR (CARN EALAR) 3276ft/994m

30 March 1964 These mountains are very remote and there are large areas of peat hag which would be extremely tedious in summer. We were lucky in having mainly good snow conditions and the lower black boggy areas were frozen.

We enjoyed the walk up Glen Tilt to the junction with Tarf Water in warm sunshine. We crossed the Tarf by the Memorial Bridge and followed this river up past the Falls for two miles. From this point we made our way across featureless snow covered slopes to the east ridge of An Sgarsoch. We saw a golden eagle. Carn an Fhidleir was another two-and-a-half miles on and involved a descent to a broad saddle between the two mountains. From this second summit we had a long and tedious descent to the Tarf through soft wet snow. We did not fancy wading the Tarf to take advantage of the short-cut over Dun Mor so we returned the same way down Glen Tilt. It had been a strenuous 9-hour day.

BEINN DEARG (Atholl) 3307ft/1008m

30 December 1966 We were camping in the Cairngorms at Glen More but the day was so vile that we drove south in search of better weather. Oliver, Christopher and I drove five miles up the very rough track from Calvine into Glen Bruar. From the car we ascended Beinn Dearg in 2 hours on a compass bearing. We went at speed because it was snowing and we had visions of being marooned with the car in the desolate glen. It was a remote area, apart from deer and ptarmigan, but below the clouds there was superb colouring from shafts of light striking the heather. The snow level was 2,000ft. Beinn Dearg is rather a featureless lump, our chief excitement was the crossing of the Bruar burn by boulder-hopping. We arrived back at Blair Atholl in time for tea, the only mishap being a damaged exhaust pipe.

CHAPTER 30

Eastern Cairngorms

LOCHNAGAR 3786ft/1155m
BROAD CAIRN 3268ft/998m

A party of us from the OUMC were staying at the splendid Lochend Bothy at the north-east corner of Loch Muick. The bothy has long since been burned out and demolished but in its day it could be a haven of comfort with a big fire roaring, stoked by logs from the small plantation nearby. It was convenient both for Lochnagar and the Dubh Loch and you could drive to the door.

20 March 1959   Alan Wedgwood and I took the path from Allt na-giubhsaich to the Meikle Pap col and traversed under the cliffs of Lochnagar. The snow conditions were fine but we were not very experienced. We climbed the left-hand branch of Black Spout Gully and to our delight broke through a small cornice to reach the summit of Lochnagar. It was our first taste of that delectable moment when, after spending some hours climbing up north facing gullies in the shade, you break out into sunshine, blue skies and space. We returned via Eagle's Rock, the Dubh Loch and mysterious Glas-allt-Shiel Lodge, peering through the windows at the retreat Queen Victoria built for herself in 1868.

21 March 1959   The next day we returned up the glen

149

to Creag an Dubh Loch and climbed the South East Gully on that impressive face. It was a natural line up a straight ribbon of snow and gave us a good climb and a double cornice at the top. Again we were lucky to emerge into sunshine on a cloudless day and we walked to the summit of Broad Cairn, only half-a-mile away, for a late lunch and a bask on a flat rock. A gentle and easy shoulder on the east side took us down to Loch Muick side.

The Lochnagar area is now a designated Wild Life Sanctuary and camping is prohibited. There is a well-marked 'preferred' route of ascent of Lochnagar via the Meikle Pap col and descent to the Glas-allt-Shiel. I consider this to be a retrograde step because walkers are now exacerbating the erosion to the paths and bulldozed tracks which scar the area. The official route is pleasant enough, but the restriction of access to this wild and fascinating group of mountains is deplorable.

I last did the 'preferred' circuit in April 1982 and, typical of post-Munro lassitude, we took with us a kettle and a Trangia stove. We brewed up at the memorial plaque under Meikle Pap, where there is a spring, and again beside the jetty at Glas-allt-Shiel. An unheard of luxury in the old days but one that I shall adopt increasingly in the years to come.

CAIRN BANNOCH 3314ft/1012m
CARN A' CHOIRE BHOIDHEACH (WHITE MOUNTH) 3630ft/1118m

25 March 1962 I climbed these peaks during the aforementioned OUMC Meet. We decided one day to walk over to Braemar for tea as the weather did not look very promising. Alan, Colin Taylor and I left for the west end of Glen Muick and Broad Cairn but, just as we reached high ground, the sky darkened and a fierce blizzard blew up. We had time to write down the necessary compass bearings on a piece of card before the snow, hail and wind arrived. The conditions were very bad indeed and we could not have used the map. After Cairn Bannoch we gave up our next summit to be, Carn an t-Sagairt Mor, and skirting the north side of Fafernie descended into upper Glen Callater. Here the wind was less and the snow had turned to heavy rain. We walked the remaining eight miles to Braemar and had our tea while standing steaming in front of a fire in the Fife Arms.

26 March 1962 The day following the storm was cold but fine and we climbed on Lochnagar again. I ascended Raeburn's Gully with Colin. There were two ice pitches and the gully gave us a hard climb. After breaking out on the summit plateau we walked over to the Stuic above the west corrie of Lochnagar and then crossed the snowy wastes of the White Mounth to reach the glen just north of Dubh Loch.

TOLMOUNT 3143ft/958m
TOM BUIDHE 3140ft/957m

7 January 1965 On yet another dull and drizzly day Oliver and I drove from Inverey to the locked gate at the entrance to Glen Callater. We walked the length of the glen to Tolmount. Unfortunately the ice on Loch Callater was too mushy to support us. Scrambling up through the fringe of cliffs we reached the summit just in time to get a bearing on Tom Buidhe before the mist closed in. These two mountains are only forty minutes apart and when the day's task was done we returned quickly to Glen Callater via a snow-filled gully. On the long walk back we were soaked again by the rain and this time Mar Lodge's central fire dried us out.

CREAG LEACACH 3238ft/987m
GLAS MAOL 3502ft/1068m
CAIRN OF CLAISE 3484ft/1064m
CARN AN TUIRC 3340ft/1019m

This group of mountains have the advantage that they can be climbed from the roadside at the top of the Devil's Elbow, a start of over 2,000ft.

5 January 1965   Oliver and I had driven up overnight and camped on snow on what turned out to be the Devil's Elbow car park. At 2 a.m., while trying to erect the tent by the light of the car headlights, we had wondered why the tent pegs wouldn't go in! It was grey and misty and the snow was soggy but we soon reached the top of Meal Odhair and rounded the shoulder of Glas Maol before following a well defined ridge to Creag Leacach. Even above 3,000ft the snow let us in to calf depth. There was no view.

From Creag Leacach we retraced our steps along the ridge and climbed to the rounded summit of Glas Maol. Two more miles across a plateau led us to Cairn of Claise but the mist became very thick and on compass bearing we overshot the col under Carn an Tuirc. Descending out of the worst of the mist we found ourselves on a spur overlooking Loch Kander and upper Glen Callater. We were able to pin-point our position and we corrected our course and reached the summit of Carn an Tuirc. We descended the steep western slopes to reach the road in steady drizzle, but the huge fire in the bar of the Fife Arms in Braemar dried us out later in the evening.

DRIESH 3105ft/947m
MAYAR 3043ft/928m
MOUNT KEEN 3077ft/939m

1 November 1969 I left Braedownie in Glen Clova at first light (7.45 a.m.) on a cold and wet morning with the cloud level down to 2,000ft. I made my way up the sodden lower slopes on to the higher ground just east of the Winter Corrie of Driesh, scrambling up beside the black precipices that looked very forbidding in the fog. By the time I reached the cairn I was soaked to the skin. An old fence then guided me down to the col on the west side and up to Mayar. I startled numerous white hares and deer. I descended from Mayar into Glen Fee by an excellent track that led through forestry plantations to Glen Doll and reached the car at 11 a.m.

A drive of 1½ hours to Glen Esk with the car's heater full on warmed me up. Glen Esk looked very lovely with the autumn colours at their best. I left the car by Loch Lee Church and followed the track up Glen Mark. The rain eased and the day improved. I had a drink from a spring at Queen's Well where a plaque recorded that Queen Victoria and the Prince Consort had visited the spot in 1861. The track, known as the Mounth Path, crosses the hills to Deeside and it took me high up on the shoulder of Mount Keen. I reached the cairn at 3 p.m. The clouds rolled back to give a tremendous panoramic view of the Eastern Cairngorms. The hills looked really golden in the winter sunshine. It had been a thoroughly enjoyable ascent of Mount Keen, the most easterly of the Munros, which from a topographical point of view is an unimpressive heather-covered mass.

CARN AN T-SAGAIRT MOR 3430ft/1047m

2 November 1969   Snow fell during the night which I spent sleeping in the car at Braemar. The morning produced a tearing wind, sleet and low cloud but I was off at 7.30 a.m. along the track up Glen Callater. The Callater burn was raging and the loch looked extremely depressing. I have never been to Glen Callater in even reasonable weather conditions. I was lucky to find an excellent stalkers' path leading well up on to the upper boulder-strewn slopes of Carn an t-Sagairt Mor. The summit plateau was snow covered and the cairn sheathed in ice. There were remains of a crashed plane near the summit. Wet and chilled I returned to the car and dry clothes at 11.15 a.m.

CHAPTER 31

Devil's Elbow

THE CAIRNWELL 3059ft/933m
CARN AOSDA 3003ft/917m
CARN A' GHEOIDH 3194ft/975m
AN SOCACH (Devil's Elbow) 3073ft/944m
GLAS TULAICHEAN 3445ft/1051m
CARN AN RIGH 3377ft/1029m
BEINN IUTHARN MHOR 3424ft/1045m
CARN BHAC 3098ft/946m

Oliver and I drove up overnight and slept under a
veranda beside the chair-lift at the top of the Devil's
Elbow. It was pouring with rain.

8 July 1967 The morning dawned fine and we were
off at 7.20 a.m. carrying a tent and food for two days.
Starting off at over 2,000ft was an extra bonus and we
had a superbly long and exhilarating day climbing eight
Munros. We did the circuit in the order listed above
and camped in the glen beyond the last one at 8 p.m.

It was a zig-zag route over high country with mixed
peat-hags, heather and soft moss. On four occasions we
were able to leave our rucksacks on a col to be collected
later. We felt rather tired on the outlying Carn an Righ
but a large tea put us right again. It was very windy
which kept the temperature down but there was a good
deal of sun and only the occasional shower. The corrie
edges were ringed with old snow. The flora was rich and
Oliver found dwarf cornel and communities of high
arctic lichen. There was a profusion of ptarmigan with

their young, many herds of deer also with young and mountain hares.

Much of the circuit of hills lie above Loch nan Eun which looked blue and inviting, there was a small tent beside it.

We camped beside the burn in Coire Bhearnaist north of Carn Bhac and the next morning walked down to Inverey.

CHAPTER 32

Glencoe and Glen Etive

MEALL DEARG 3118ft/953m
SGOR NAM FIANNAIDH 3168ft/967m

16 April 1965 These two Munros lie on the north side of Glencoe and the sharp serrated ridge between them is called the Aonach Eagach. This ridge has a formidable reputation and there is no easy way off on either side once you are committed.

Nigel Rogers and I traversed the ridge in four hours from the Meeting of Three Waters (on the main road) to the Clachaig Hotel. We ascended Am Bodach on a lovely warm spring day; there was very little snow but just some verglas early on. On the main ridge we were in shirt-sleeves and made good speed and nowhere did we find any difficulties. It was easy to see though that under winter conditions the ridge would be a completely different proposition.

We descended beside Clachaig Gully which splits Sgor nam Fiannaidh for 1,500ft. The gully provides one of Glencoe's and indeed Scotland's classic climbs. A year later I returned and with Oliver [Gilbert] climbed the gully. It took us 5 hours in pouring rain and it thoroughly lived up to its reputation. The rain made the rocks greasy but, apart from that, it did not matter much as a waterfall pitch quite near the bottom soaked us completely. We found no definite crux on the climb but six or seven pitches were testing without being gripping!

SGORR DHONUILL 3284ft/1001m
SGORR DHEARG 3362ft/1024m

21 April 1965   These two Munros make up the group known as Beinn a' Bheithir and they are very conspicuous, rising above the Ballachulish Hotel as one waits for the ferry on the north side. The north-facing slopes are afforested, but above the trees the main ridge makes a perfect horseshoe with the rocky nose of Sgorr a' Chaolais prominent in the centre.

I climbed the group alone one morning leaving Ballachulish Hotel at 6.30 a.m. I climbed the ridge over Sgorr a' Chaolais and found it required quite a hard rock scramble. I found purple mountain saxifrage just below the snow line at 2,700ft. As I reached the summit of Sgorr Dhonuill the clouds were dispersing rapidly and the view began to unfold all round. The Mamores, Bidean nam Bian and the Glen Creran group looked magnificent capped with snow against the blue sky.

I continued east along the ridge to Sgorr Dhearg and descended over the subsidiary summit of Sgorr Bhan marked 3104 on the map. From there I scrambled down to Glen Guibhsachain and reached the road one mile east of Ballachulish Hotel at 12.30 p.m.

BUACHAILLE ETIVE MOR 3345ft/1022m

3 October 1965   I must have passed this impressive cone of rock standing at the upper entrance to Glencoe many dozens of times before stopping long enough to climb it.

With Oliver on a damp October's day. We crossed the Coupal River by the stepping stones, just under water, and slogged up the marshy path to Rannoch Wall. We climbed Agag's Groove route in four long pitches. It was a splendid introduction to rock climbing on the Buachaille and there were many wonderful positions and the route was very exposed. The rock was wet and we found the crux to be on the first pitch. It was drizzling throughout.

We continued up Crowberry Ridge to the summit and then descended quickly down Curved Ridge as the weather closed in.

BEN STARAV 3541ft/1078m
BUACHAILLE ETIVE BEAG 3130ft/958m
STOB COIR 'AN ALBANNAICH 3425ft/1044m

17 December 1962 Trisha and I were staying at Inbirfhaolain, the attractive club hut in Glen Etive.

We climbed the shapely peak of Ben Starav by the north ridge. The ridge is easy-angled and pleasant and becomes sharp near the top. It was misty and there were flurries of snow so we did not go on to Glas Bheinn Mhor. We were followed most of the way up and down by two goats who at the end of the day seemed quite bedraggled and exhausted. We took them to Coileitir Farm where we were sat in front of the fire and given tea. The goats had been lost for several weeks. The farmer was busy collecting holly, which grew in profusion on the lower crags, and despatching it to Glasgow for the Christmas market.

18 December 1962 The next day was bad, blizzardy weather. We wrapped up well and made a quick dash up and down Stob Dubh on Buachaille Etive Beag. We struggled through deep snow on the south ridge from Dalness. It completed the day's Munro but had nothing else to recommend it in the conditions.

19 December 1962 During the night conditions changed completely and we woke to a fine clear and sunny day. For the first time we could see Bidean, Ben Cruachan and Stob Ghabhar.

We crossed the River Etive by the bridge near Coileitir and climbed Stob Coir 'an Albannaich by the broad north-west ridge. It took us 3 hours of difficult going to reach the summit, firstly up steep, heathery slopes under deep snow and higher up across a plateau, still through deep, uncompacted snow. However, the day was superb and I have never seen the Highlands looking better; the setting of dazzling white mountains against a blue sky cannot be beaten.

We ploughed down through the snow northwards to the col under Meall Tarsuinn and returned to Coileitir alongside the Allt Ceitlein, leaving Meall nan Eun for another day.

MEALL NAN EUN 3039ft/928m

14 March 1963 The fact that I had missed climbing Meall nan Eun when very close to the summit the previous December had been on my mind ever since. I took the opportunity of remedying this on a dark and wet March day when my wife preferred to sit reading in the comfortable lounge of the Kingshouse Hotel. I crossed the River Etive by the Coileitir Farm bridge and ascended the north-west ridge through wet snow. It was a most unattractive mountain, climbed on an abominable day. 4 hours round trip from the road.

BEINN NAN AIGHENAN 3141ft/957m
GLAS BHEINN MHOR 3258ft/997m

15 August 1966 Oliver and I were camping near Forest Lodge beside Loch Tulla. The sunrise woke us at 5.30 a.m. and we found ice particles inside the tent, where our breath had frozen, and a heavy hoar frost outside.

It had been a still clear night and throughout the day the sun blazed down from a cloudless sky.

After a midgy breakfast we struck camp and left at 8.30 a.m., Oliver to survey the lichen round the Fort William Aluminium Works and I to walk over the tops to Glen Etive and then hitch round to Fort William.

I had a most enjoyable walk to the upper reaches of Glen Kinglass passing beneath the southern slopes of Stob Ghabhar, Meall nan Eun and Stob Coir 'an Albannaich. After 2 hours I struck up the long east ridge of Beinn nan Aighenan and passed within ten yards of three young stags grazing on the moss.

Beinn nan Aighenan provided an excellent viewpoint for Ben Cruachan and Ben Starav. I descended 1000ft to the north and then climbed up again to meet the Ben Starav – Glas Bheinn Mhor ridge. As I breasted the ridge I saw, in a hollow, three deerstalkers with the correct head-gear, rifles and spy glasses. By a miracle they did not see me, I would not have been popular, so I hurried on to the summit of Glas Bheinn Mhor for lunch.

It was very hot and I was unfit so I ambled down to the col under Stob Coir 'an Albannaich and then descended to Coileitir Farm in Glen Etive. I reached the road at 4 p.m., soon picked up a lift and was in Fort William 2 hours later.

CHAPTER 33

Black Mount

MEALL A' BHUIRIDH 3636ft/1108m
CLACH LEATHAD (CLACHLET) 3602ft/1100m
STOB GHABHAR 3565ft/1087m
STOB A' CHOIRE ODHAIR 3058ft/943m

17 March 1963 On an overcast and drizzly day I left
Trisha skiing on Meall a' Bhuiridh and walked on past
the chair-lifts and drags to the summit. Using the
compass I followed the ridge round to Clach Leathad
and then descended out of the mist to Bealach Fuar-
chathaidh. This area is a complex one with ridges,
subsidiary ridges and cols abounding and it was a great
help to be able to see my way up on to the big ridge
called Aonach Mor that leads to the summit of Stob
Ghabhar.

I was sorry to be on Stob Ghabhar in such poor
conditions as it is one of the great mountains of the
Scottish Highlands. It is easily recognisable by its
magnificent upper couloir on the eastern side which
carries snow late into the spring, and I have seen and
admired it on many occasions from peaks near and far.

I descended the east ridge until I was under the small
shapely peak of Stob a' Choire Odhair. I made a
mammoth effort and traversed it on my way back to
Forest Lodge. I was tired and unfit and I had pulled a
muscle in my thigh but I limped back to the Bridge of
Orchy Hotel where my wife met me with the car. 8

hours from Kingshouse to Bridge of Orchy.

Another enjoyable traverse of the Black Mount hills can be made from Coupall Bridge, near the entrance to Glen Etive, to Bridge of Orchy. This walk misses out Meall a'Bhuirdh but includes the ascent of the splendid, shapely peak of Sron na Creise, which is seen from Kingshouse, rising dramatically from the flat moors.

On my second visit to the Black Mount, in April 1981, I was quite happy to forego Meall a'Bhuirdh with its ski-tows, cafes and other paraphernalia and take this alternative route.

Gerard Simpson and I much enjoyed the scramble up the steep north ridge of Sron na Creise and the walk along the broad corniced ridge to Clachlet. On this occasion Clachlet and Stob Ghabhar were out of cloud and we could fully understand their high reputation amongst hill-walkers.

A narrow and shattered rock ridge leads down from the eastern shoulder of Stob Ghabhar to the bealach under Stob a' Choire Odhair. We left this latter mountain alone and preferred the easy descent beside the Allt Toaig to the Linne nam Beathach and the Land Rover track to Forest Lodge. Luckily, two climbers who had left their car at Forest Lodge, gave us a lift to Bridge of Orchy whence we hitched back to Glen Etive. 7 hours from Coupall Bridge to Forest Lodge.

CHAPTER 34

Ben Cruachan

BEN CRUACHAN 3689ft/1126m
STOB DIAMH 3272ft/998m
BEINN A' CHOCHUILL 3215ft/980m
BEINN EUNAICH 3242ft/989m
SGOR NA H-ULAIDH 3258ft/994m
BEINN FHIONNLAIDH (Argyll) 3139ft/959m
BEINN SGULAIRD 3059ft/937m

13 December 1963 Trisha and I spent a few days at the splendid Loch Awe Hotel. With its oak-panelled hall, wide stairs and stags' heads it was traditionally Scottish as was the hospitality, particularly as we were very nearly the only residents.

We drove some way up the new access road to the Cruachan hydroelectric scheme which was being built at this time. The whole area was devastated by the attack of man and machine and we were depressed by this intrusion. If pumped-storage schemes become popular the Highlands will be threatened again, because they need high lakes, and if no natural ones exist in the right places artificial ones will be made.

The snow level was 2,000ft and we continued together to the main ridge of Cruachan before Trisha returned, sensibly as she was six months pregnant. It was a fine clear day and it was wonderful to be back in Scotland again after a five months absence. We could easily see across to Mull and Ben More and the Ben Lui group was prominent to the east.

I had a most enjoyable traverse of Ben Cruachan and had to cut a few steps where the snow was hard and icy. After Stob Diamh I had to lose 1,500ft to the col under Beinn a' Chochuill but, having made up the height again, the ridge continued easily to Beinn Eunaich which I reached at 3.45 p.m. There was a lovely sunset looking back beyond Cruachan to Mull. It was a quick and easy descent down the southern slopes to Loch Awe.

14 December 1963 The next day was another crisp and fine winter's day with a hard frost. I drove round to the head of Glen Creran and climbed Sgor na h-Ulaidh by the very steep south-west ridge. I found the ridge very difficult near the top and had to hack out some steps in the slippery frozen grass-cum-scree. At the top I was rewarded by extensive views all round, Ben Nevis, Bidean, Stob Ghabhar, Cruachan and the Mamores. I descended steeply to the col on the south side and climbed Beinn Fhionnlaidh which also involved some steep scrambling. It was now getting dark quickly and I hastened down to Glen Creran. A golden eagle glided to within a few yards of me as I ran down a scree gully. The western sky was aglow with a deep red sunset.

15 December 1963 The following day the weather was changing and it was grey and threatening but I decided to go out to climb Beinn Sgulaird, the last of the three Munros accessible from Glen Creran. From Elleric I ascended the north-western slopes quickly as it is a very easily climbed mountain. 2 hours 50 minutes up and down.

I returned to Ben Cruachan on 30 October 1980 when Gerard Simpson and Basil Postlethwaite and I spent rather a humiliating day on the mountain.

The morning started clear and frosty and, having parked at the bottom of the dam access road near the Loch Awe Hotel, we made good speed to the upper reservoir. Grassy slopes led easily towards Meall Cuanail, but we made the bad decision to traverse steep broken ground to gain the bealach under Cruachan's 3689ft main peak. The scree was verglassed and rimed and horribly slippery.

As we proceeded east towards Stob Diamh, thick freezing mist enveloped us and at point 3312ft (Drochaid Glas) we took the wrong (north) ridge. Unfortunately we had no compass, for each had assumed the other had taken one with him! After about 10 minutes we suspected that we were wrong and returned to point 3312. Once again, though, we could see no other obvious ridge descending, apart from a steep spur on the left – possibly the north ridge? Thus we assumed we had been right all along and we returned down our original ridge.

We must have descended about 800ft before we emerged out of the mist, and the lie of the land below made it obvious that we were completely off course. For the third time we toiled up to point 3312 and this time located the ridge leading to Stob Diamh. I should warn prospective walkers that no actual ridge is visible, but as you descend the loose rocky slopes a faint path with some small marker cairns materialises.

From Stob Diamh the descent to the reservoir was uneventful and we finally reached the car after a 7 hour day. Our blunders must have cost us 2 hours.

In retrospect, it was a good example of Murphy's Law. 'Experience is directly proportional to the cost of equipment lost or damaged or to the inconvenience suffered.'

CHAPTER 35

Mull

BEN MORE (Mull) 3169ft/966m

30 January 1971 The one-day expedition from the mainland to Mull that Christopher and I made to climb Ben More ranks as one of my very best days in Scotland. If I had not been doing the Munros I would never have undertaken such a scheme and therefore would have missed this eventful and rewarding day.

We drove up to Oban on the Friday evening and arrived at 12.30 a.m. The roads beyond Tyndrum were covered with packed snow, it was a clear starry night and very cold. I fell flat on my face on the quayside which was glazed with ice but it was a relief to leave the car and enjoy the clean air and smell of the sea

Our plan was to catch the morning ferry to Craignure, proceed to Ben More by bus and foot and to return by the last ferry at 4.30 p.m. Timing was vital as, there being no Sunday ferry, the next one was on the Monday when we were due back at work.

The Columba sailed at 6.30 a.m. and we enjoyed an excellent breakfast of porridge, kippers and coffee. Our appetite was not spoiled by two workmen sitting opposite discussing the inadequate sewers of Oban.

The local bus dropped us at Salen at 8.10 a.m. and we set out along the road past Gruline and Knock towards Ben More. The road was very icy but the day dawned a beauty. Loch na Keall and west to Ulva was bright in the sunshine and we saw many and varied seabirds. A few snowdrops were out near Mac Quarrie's Mausoleum. It was a day in a million.

We left the road six-and-a-half miles beyond Salen and crossed Glen na Beinn Fada to reach the upper slopes of Ben More and the cairn at 12.15. There was fresh powder snow above 800ft, quite deep high up and the rocks were glazed with ice. The wind was streaming powder snow over the ridge. We were in shadow during our ascent up the northern slopes but on the summit the sun hit us and we enjoyed 10 minutes of the greatest exhilaration. There were extensive views all round the compass, Ben Cruachan, Gharb-Bheinn of Ardgour, the Cuillins white with snow and beneath us, the islands of Ulva, Little Colonsay and Staffa. A most attractive looking ridge continued round to A'Chioch but unfortunately we did not have time to take it.

We were slightly behind schedule so we turned round and sped off down passing a herd of deer and two arctic hares in the glen. Back on the road we had six-and-a-half miles to cover in 1¼ hours or miss the bus at Salen, and the ferry and be marooned till Monday. Christopher was somewhat out of condition and with 25 minutes and two and a half miles to go we were feeling rather desperate, particularly as no car had passed us on the road. Just at that moment however a car appeared and lifted us to Salen, and from there another lift took us to Craignure, and at 4 p.m. we were enjoying tea on the Columba.

Travelling 700 miles for a very few hours on Ben More sounds ridiculous but for us it was highly satisfying and hugely enjoyable.

CHAPTER 36

Beinn Laoigh

BEINN LAOIGH (BEN LUI) 3708ft/1130m
BEINN OSS 3374ft/1029m
BEINN DUBHCHRAIG 3204ft/978m
BEINN A' CHLEIBH 3008ft/916m

1 March 1964   Richard Gowing and I drove along the
very rough road to Cononish Farm under Ben Lui
(Laoigh). It was a beautiful day, crisp and frozen
underfoot yet the sun warm on our necks. We climbed
the classic Central Gully which gave us a magnificent
900ft snow climb. We were able to kick steps up the
first 400ft but thereafter the angle increased and we
roped up, cutting steps for extra security although we
were wearing crampons. The cornice was only a thin lip
and we arrived on the sundrenched summit ridge only
ten yards from the cairn.

It was satisfying to have climbed the mountain by
such a direct route and the climb justified its reputation.
Nowhere was the angle excessive yet exposure was ever
present and I could see the danger of avalanche in bad
conditions. In fact Richard and a large party had been
avalanched the previous Easter, luckily with no serious
consequences.

We walked round the ridge to Beinn Oss but a thick
mist rolled in and we got lost in trying to find the
summit of Beinn Dubhchraig. We must have been very
near the cairn at times, but we never found it; the

ground was rocky and hummocky and there were several lochans not marked on the map. After an hour's fruitless blundering about we gave up the search and hastened down out of the mist to the car.

2 November 1968 I returned to the Ben Lui group on a wonderfully clear and sunny November's day in 1968. Alone I walked in from the main road a mile south of Tyndrum and climbed the entire group of Bens Dubhchraig, Oss, Lui and a' Chleibh in 7¾ hours to the Dalmally road.

The wind was strong and there was fresh snow above 2,000ft. Strangely there was dead calm at the summit of Ben Lui. The rocky ridges were festooned in green ice, a phenomenon that I have never seen since.

It is a very pleasant high-level walk but for me the day was made by the sunshine, the blue skies and the tremendous views. This day coming after one of winter blizzards which I had spent in the upper Glen Lyon group of mountains.

I repeated this traverse in early April 1973 with Oliver Gilbert and Paul Hawksworth on a day of arctic conditions. It was a superb Scottish winter's day with powdered snow drifts and ice and the occasional squall of snow. We had sunshine too and magnificent views ranging from Ben More to Ben Cruachan and north to the Mamores, all gleaming white with fresh snow.

CHAPTER 37

Bridge of Orchy

BEINN DORAIN 3524ft/1074m
BEINN MHANACH 3125ft/954m
BEINN AN DOTHAIDH 3283ft/1002m

10 January 1970 Christopher and I left Bridge of Orchy on an overcast day with low clouds. A thaw had just set in after a week of snow and very low temperatures, −16°c had been recorded in Glasgow two days previously. The hills were streaked with snow and most of the burns were choked with ice and just beginning to flow again.

We climbed straight up to meet the north ridge of Beinn Dorain. It was icy and we needed to kick steps in the snow. At 2,000ft we were in mist, but on the broad ridge the snow was frozen and gave easy walking and we reached the cairn after 2 hours.

The visibility was no more than ten yards but by compass we found our way down Coire a' Ghabhalach. We stopped for lunch of cold sausages and Christmas cake just below cloud-level under Beinn a' Chuirn.

A rough and ice-sheeted track led towards Loch Lyon. We left the track at the watershed and climbed up through the mist again to Beinn Mhanach. It must be a good viewpoint in clear weather but today it was just another snowy peak in the icy grip of winter. The grass low down was hard and slippery and the rocks above were encased in feathery frost. We returned down the Auch Glen and the Allt Charoghlais was frozen across and bearing. From the viaduct we walked back to the car along three-and-a-half miles of railway line as darkness fell. An 8½ hour day and quite long enough in our state of unfitness.

11 January 1970 The next morning the day seemed more promising, the cloud level was higher and patches of blue sky were appearing at intervals. We left Bridge of Orchy at first light and climbed the west ridge of Beinn an Dothaidh reaching the cairn after 2 hours.

Unfortunately we were once again in thick mist and we used the compass to find our way to the steep slopes leading down to the Achaladair col. After descending a few hundred feet through the mist with crags on each side, the going became extremely unpleasant. Below us the slope continued steeper than ever and became badly iced. We cut steps down for a further 200ft or so before discretion prevailed and we retreated. The ground was so steep, frozen and ice-covered that an ice-axe would probably not have arrested a slip. It was a thoroughly dangerous place and with much relief we ate our lunch on the easier ground above.

The east-facing cliffs were heavily corniced and the visibility was atrocious. As we were now too late to complete the Achaladair–Chreachain ridge we retraced our footsteps and ambled our way back down to Bridge of Orchy.

BEINN ACHALADAIR 3404ft/1039m
BEINN A' CHREACHAIN 3540ft/1081m

16 December 1970 On a mild but grey December day Paul Hawksworth and I parked the car near Achallader Farm and walked up to the col between Beinn an

Dothaidh and Beinn Achaladair. We traversed Beinn Achaladair and Beinn a' Chreachain on compass bearing all day, but managed occasional glimpses across Loch Tulla to Stob Ghabhar.

There was very little snow on the southern slopes but the northern corries were full and the main ridge corniced. In the mist we couldn't find an easy way off Beinn a' Chreachain and so we descended in a southerly direction first and then traversed round to meet the railway line not far from Gorton. It was a long walk back along the line and the wind was rising to gale force and a storm was imminent. We made it back to the car just before the storm broke.

CHAPTER 38

Glen Lyon

SCHIEHALLION 3547ft/1083m
CREAG MHOR (Carn Mairg) 3200ft/981m
CARN MAIRG 3419ft/1042m
MEALL GARBH (Carn Mairg) 3200ft/963m
CARN GORM 3370ft/1029m
BEN CHONZIE 3048ft/931m

3 August 1963 Trisha and I ambled up Schiehallion on a beautiful summer afternoon with the heather just coming out. We left the car at the top of the small road that runs south from Kinloch Rannoch and passes under the northern slopes of the mountain. This gives a start of over 1,000ft.

Schiehallion, from many directions, is a perfect cone and as such is easily recognised from afar.

4 August 1963 The following day I spent alone in misty weather on the Carn Mairg range. I left the road two miles west of Fortingall at 8 a.m. and made my way up the heather covered slopes just behind a large farm. I was, I suppose, about half a mile beyond the farm when pandemonium broke loose behind me. With frenzied barking about four or five huge Alsatian dogs were flat out in pursuit of me. I am not a dog lover at the best of times and I could imagine the farmer thought I was a poacher and had sent the dogs to tear me to pieces.

I was terrified. I literally ran up those steep slopes

through the deep heather until, sick and faint with exhaustion, I collapsed. I was just out of sight of the farm and in thin mist, there was no sign of the dogs.

I spent the rest of the day walking over the high broad plateau that makes up the range while I slowly unwound. I was still un-nerved as my heart leapt when a stag appeared suddenly out of the mist and I thought back to the report I had read of a gamekeeper being gored to death by a stag in November 1889.

The sun came out on Carn Gorm to give me a hot and midgy descent to Inverar.

5 August 1963 We camped the night near Auchnafree in upper Glen Almond. It was a damp and drizzly morning so I made a quick ascent alone of Ben Chonzie. 2 hours and 10 minutes up and down.

I returned to Ben Chonzie in April 1973 on a glorious early spring day. Again from upper Glen Almond but after a sharp frost which left the river with a skin of ice at the edge. From the col on the eastern shoulder an old fence leads up to the summit cairn. There was deep powder snow on the upper slopes but it was warm enough in the sunshine to have a long lie by the cairn.

Ben Chonzie makes a good half day's expedition on a drive south from the Highlands.

MEALL BUIDHE (Glen Lyon) 3054ft/931m
STUCHD AN LOCHAIN 3144ft/960m

I drove up to Scotland on the evening of 31 October in the teeth of a severe blizzard. The wind was shipping snow and sleet across the roads and the mountains were white. I spent a cold night in the car parked under the Loch Giorra dam at the head of Glen Lyon, and on such a night I did not sleep peacefully with the thought of those millions of gallons poised above me.

1 November 1968   At 8.30 a.m. the next morning I left for Meall Buidhe wrapped in three jerseys, anorak and cagoule. Stags from several herds were belling as the deer were forced down by the conditions. After 30 minutes I fell through the snow up to my waist in frozen bog. It was so cold that my socks and breeches froze to armour at once but I had to suffer frozen feet all day. My toes were slightly frostbitten as I had no feeling in them for the next two months.

The snow was powdery and between ankle and knee deep, I wished for my ice-axe and snow-gaiters which I had left at home. The tearing north-east wind was full gale force and on the final ridge was almost too much to bear with the whirling snow flakes and ice spicules. Visibility however was reasonable and I could see right down the north-facing corrie to Loch Rannoch.

I was back at the dam by 11.30 a.m. and started straight away for Stuchd an Lochain on the south side of Loch Giorra. It was a constant struggle against the deep snow, fantastic wind and, near the top, cramp and snowblindness. I made my way up to the col between the main mountain and the subsidiary Creag an Fheadain and followed an easy ridge round to the summit.

On my drive south from Glen Lyon I followed Land Rover tracks and just made it across the high road between Bridge of Balgie and Loch Tay through snow that was a foot deep in places.

CHAPTER 39

Glen Lochay

SGIATH CHUIL 3050ft/935m
MEALL GLAS 3139ft/960m
BEINN CHALLUM 3354ft/1025m
BEINN HEASGARNICH 3530ft/1076m
CREAG MHOR (Loch Lyon) 3387ft/1032m

It was a wild and wet evening as I drove through Killin on my way to Glen Lochay. The Dochart river was roaring and foaming under the bridge and I decided not to put up a tent so I slept in the car near Kenknock.

27 March 1968 The next morning curtains of rain were sweeping down the glen driven by a high wind and the Lochay river was in full flood and had burst its banks.

Later in the morning I braved the elements and climbed Sgiath Chuil from the bridge over the river at Lubchurran. I was not able to cross the Allt Innisdaimh burn below about 2,250ft. as it was in full spate. It was a real battle along the ridge between Meall a' Churain and Sgiath Chuil in dreadful conditions with sheeting rain.

I descended towards Meall Glas down a long tongue of snow but once on the peat-hag ridden watershed with water, slush and thick mist everywhere I gave up for the day. Both my legs were numb from repeated immersions up to the knees in icy bogs and I was not very fit.

177

I returned to Glen Lochay and the car, again crossing the river by the suspension bridge at Lubchurran. It was still pouring and I had been on compass bearing all day. I learned later that Fort William had recorded a record of 5 inches of rain during those 24 hours.

28 March 1968 The following morning I left for another attempt on Meall Glas. It was still raining but the wind was less fierce. From Lubchurran I struck diagonally across the sodden hillsides towards Beinn Cheathaich which lies one mile to the east of Meall Glas. I kicked steps up the last few hundred feet to reach the broad summit ridge and soon gained the Meall Glas cairn.

Descending westwards from the summit I reached the Lochay river at the 1,000ft. level and I had a very nasty time crossing it with the water well above my knees. Beyond the river I had a 2-hour slog up the east ridge of Beinn Challum. It was a mixture of steep snow slopes and rocky outcrops. Once again I had no sort of view from the summit and the compass was in use all day.

Luckily the descent down the north side to the Allt Challum was a 2,000ft. snow-run and I soon reached a good track at the deserted buildings of Batavaime. It was a further three miles to the car, the day's expedition having taken 7½ hours. The rain stopped during the afternoon and I had hopes of a general improvement in the weather for the next day.

29 March 1968 I was still optimistic the next morning for the peaks were out of cloud early on. I drove to Badour and made my way up the southern slopes of Beinn Heasgarnich. Before long however the clouds came down and the inevitable compass came out. I reached the ridge between the main summit and the subsidiary summit of Stob an Fhir-Bhogha and soon located the cairn. I returned to the latter summit and then descended the south-west ridge to beneath Creag Mhor. After lunch on the col it took me an hour to climb the steep snow and rock-covered slopes to Creag Mhor summit but again the descent south was an easy snow-run. Unfortunately I came down too far west and had a long and tedious traverse to regain the track at Batavaime. A 5½ hour day.

The weather had been really abysmal for three days and the visibility on the five summits was never more than twenty yards.

CHAPTER 40

Ben Lawers and the Tarmachans

BEN LAWERS 3984ft/1214m
MEALL CORRANAICH 3530ft/1069m
MEALL A' CHOIRE LEITH 3033ft/926m
BEINN GHLAS 3657ft/1103m
MEALL GREIGH 3280ft/1001m
MEALL GARBH (Ben Lawers) 3661ft/1118m

16 August 1951 Ben Lawers was the first Munro I ever climbed, I was 13 and on a family holiday at Ardeonaig on the south side of Loch Tay. I remember that we walked up from Lawers village and were impressed by the flora; one of my brothers was a keen botanist. We climbed to the top of the huge cairn and reckoned that our heads were above 4,000ft. I have always had a place near my heart for Ben Lawers and I try and identify it from other mountains. The Lawers range provides excellent walking and the mountains are mostly grassy and connected by undulating ridges, not unlike the Fannich mountains.

8 January 1965 I was next back in the Lawers range on a cold January day with Oliver, Richard Gowing and Patrick Duncan. From Lochan na Lairige we traversed Meall Corranaich and Meall a' Choire Leith. We saw an arctic hare and the next moment a golden eagle dropped from the sky and grasped the unfortunate animal in its claws, as we exclaimed the eagle took fright and soared off over the ridge.

The snow conditions were good, we could mostly kick steps and only had to use the axes where the surface was hard and icy. Even the sun came out for a few minutes and we saw the Brocken Spectre. At regular intervals squalls of snow blew up but all in all it was a splendid Scottish winter day.

10 January 1965 Two days later the weather was appalling with very low cloud and heavy rain. Bearing in mind that the previous day we had spent on Meall Ghaordie had improved dramatically as the morning progressed we set off from Loch Tay for Beinn Ghlas. Unfortunately the opposite occurred and the steady rain turned to torrential downpour. Accurate compass work brought us to the summit of Beinn Ghlas but in the atrocious conditions it took us 25 minutes to find the cairn. The wind and freezing rain brought back memories of Sgurr na Ciche, but once we had located the cairn it did not take us long to run down to better conditions below.

18 August 1966 Oliver and I left Lawers village on a warm sunny day for the Lawers range. We walked over Meall Greigh and Meall Garbh where Oliver found some rare lichens and we lunched on the summit of Ben Lawers. It was so good to have the time and weather to lounge on a high peak enjoying life. We found alpine forgetmenot, drooping saxifrage and saxifrage nivalis.

On the way down it was hot and sultry and we bathed in a pool near a huge concrete pipe laid by the hydroelectric authorities.

The contrast in weather could hardly have been greater on 30 October 1981 when Gerard Simpson and I traversed the Lawers range in full winter conditions.

Leaving the monstrous National Trust Visitors' Centre on the high road over to Glen Lyon, we struggled through knee-deep snow over Beinn Ghlas and on to Ben Lawers where we could scarcely stand against the wind and blown spindrift. The clouds parted at intervals to give bright sun and blue skies and the mountains were magnificent in their coats of white.

The descent from An Stuc to the Meall Garbh bealach through very steep and deep powder-snow was quite tricky, and ploughing over Meall Greigh was exhausting. Lawers village reached after 6¼ hours.

MEALL NAN TARMACHAN 3421ft/1043m
MEALL GHAORDIE 3407ft/1039m

27 March 1964   I climbed the highest Tarmachan with my brothers. We started from Lochan na Lairige by the high road between Loch Tay and Glen Lyon. It was very misty with deep slushy snow on the hills and we needed the compass to find Meall nan Tarmachan. The ascent was easy and in 2 hours we were at the cairn having followed footprints in the snow over the last stretch. The conditions did not encourage us to continue along the ridge so we retraced our steps.

9 January 1965   Oliver, Patrick Duncan, Richard Gowing and I were camping at Killin. We spent most of the morning in the cafe as the clouds were down and it was sleeting. However we were determined to achieve something and so we drove to Glen Lochay and made an enjoyable ascent of Meall Ghaordie from Tullich. On the upper slopes there was deep fresh powder snow with several icy areas blown clear by the wind. The clouds rolled back and the sun emerged but the wind was fierce so after reaching the cairn we tumbled down through the snow to the road. We ate a late lunch beside the River Lochay in warm sunshine.

CHAPTER 41

The Crianlarich Hills and Ben Vorlich

BEN MORE (Crianlarich) 3843ft/1174m
STOB BINNEIN (STOBINIAN) 3827ft/1165m
CRUACH ARDRAIN 3428ft/1046m
BEINN TULAICHEAN 3099ft/946m

29 February 1964   Richard Gowing and I climbed Ben More from Benmore farm at the base of the north-west ridge. There was snow only above about 2,500ft and conditions were good. 2 hours to the summit. There were thin wisps of cloud that let the sunshine through at times and a gusty wind which blew the powder snow in whirls.

We continued on over Stob Binnein and then descended 2,200ft to the col below Stob Garbh for lunch in a sheltered spot out of the wind.

Cruach Ardrain looked enormous, towering above us into the clouds in a perfect cone. It was exciting too and we had to cut steps up a steep couloir near the top of the east face. We continued on southwards along the ridge to Beinn Tulaichean before descending to the glen. It was a long but pleasant walk back down Benmore Glen with Ben More and Stobinian now clear of mist, snow capped and pink in the setting sun.

I was back in this area in the first week of April 1973 with Oliver and a party of senior boys from Ampleforth College Mountaineering Club. We were refused permission to approach Ben More because recent wreckage from a crashed Vanguard aeroplane had not yet been cleared from the summit.

We drove round to Glen Falloch and walked in along the river Falloch. The weather was wintry and we skirted Stob Glas and made for Beinn Tulaichean in a snowstorm with a gale force wind that cut us to the bone. In spite of full heavy winter clothing I was soon frozen.

The mountains were incredible, either deep powder-snow, snow-ice or bare ice bulges over the rocks and grass. After Tulaichean we climbed Cruach Ardrain and the storm passed on leaving blue skies with plumes of snow streaming off Stob Binnein and Ben More in the high wind.

The descent to the col under Stob Binnein was steep and treacherous with much powder-snow over ice. Oliver descended with some difficulty and he traversed Stob Binnein and afterwards reported fantastic winter conditions and a high wind which blew him over at times. The rest of us had a gentle and enjoyable descent by the north-west ridge over Meall Dhamh.

It was one of the severest yet most enjoyable days I have experienced. The conditions were truly arctic and challenging yet the late appearance of the sun made up for the earlier storm.

BEN VORLICH (Loch Earn) 3224ft/985m
STUC A' CHROIN 3189ft/975m
BEINN CHABHAIR 3053ft/933m
AN CAISTEAL 3265ft/995m
BEINN A' CHROIN 3104ft/946m

13 March 1965 Richard Gowing and I were camping near Blaircreich farm at the head of Balquhidder. After a fine frosty night and sunny dawn we left for Loch Earn-side hoping for a snow climb on the cliffs of Stuc a' Chroin.

We first climbed up Ben Vorlich by the north ridge from Ardvorlich. There was a good deal of snow above 1,500ft but it was very soft and we gave up hope of climbing on Stuc a' Chroin. However we descended to the low col under Stuc a' Chroin and scrambled up some steep rocks to the summit. The weather had deteriorated and it was now raining so we hastened back to the car down Glen Ample and dried out over tea in the Lochearnhead Hotel.

14 March 1965 The following morning was still overcast and drizzly but we hoped for the best and from the head of Balquhidder we systematically climbed Beinn Chabhair, An Caisteal and Beinn a' Chroin. Unfortunately the weather did not improve and we were on compass bearings in thick mist all day. The mountains are shapely and make a compact little group with low cols dividing one from another. They would make a delightful day in clear weather but on this occasion we were glad to return to the car, drenched, at tea time.

CHAPTER 42

Loch Lomond and Arrochar

BEN VORLICH (Loch Lomond) 3092ft/943m
BEN VANE 3004ft/915m

5 December 1964 Oliver, Christopher and I were camping at Inveruglas by Loch Lomond. It was a raw wet morning and the snow level was down to 1,000ft., but we ascended Ben Vorlich through thick mist on compass bearing via the south ridge.

We descended the steep western slopes to the Loch Sloy dam. In places there were ice bulges and frozen waterfalls which required careful negotiation.

We ate lunch cowering under a concrete awning while it rained harder than ever. Another Munro was very near however, so we made a quick dash up and down Ben Vane following our own footsteps in the snow. It had been rather a depressing day and it was dark and we were soaked by the time we reached camp again.

BEINN NARNAIN 3036ft/926m
BEINN IME 3318ft/1011m
BEINN BHUIDHE 3106ft/948m
BEN LOMOND 3192ft/974m

26 June 1965 Finding myself free in Glasgow on a Saturday lunchtime and with a day-and-a-half at my disposal I decided to explore the Arrochar range and other mountains of the Southern Highlands. Although I was successful from a Munro climbing point of view I was much too hasty to take in and to appreciate the hills, and I am determined to return with more time at my disposal.

I drove through Arrochar and left the car a mile from the Rest and be Thankful road junction. I climbed Beinn Narnain and Beinn Ime from the Bealach a' Mhaim. The going was very easy and although it was overcast I had excellent views of the Cobbler. The round trip took 3 hours.

Then from the road west of Beinn an Lochain I climbed this mountain via its steep and tedious south ridge. Near the summit there were some deep holes on the ridge, some crater type and some honeycombed. This is a very accessible mountain and I was back on the road in less than 2 hours. (Following a resurvey, Beinn an Lochain was removed from Munro's Tables.)

It was now evening and I drove into Inveraray for dinner. Later as it was still dry, and the weather looked promising and as I was feeling fit after an excellent meal, I decided to walk up Beinn Bhuidhe.

I drove up the private road along Glen Shira as far as the point where the power cables cross. Luckily the gates were not locked, in spite of notices to the contrary. At 9.40 p.m. I left the car and in ever-fading light made good speed up the south-west ridge of Beinn Bhuidhe. By 11 p.m. it was almost dark but when looking back against the western sky I could just make out the silhouette of the ridge. By the latter method and by using my luminous compass (I had not brought a torch) I remained on course. The slope was little help because of numerous false summits. I arrived at the summit trig point at 11.15 p.m. after an exciting ascent for I found that being alone on a mountain at night heightened all my senses. It was my first experience of this. Had I missed the summit cairn I would have bivouacked until first light.

On the descent it seemed to be darker still and I found it difficult deciding whether my foot was being placed on flat ground, sloping ground or in a peat-hag. Anyway, I stumbled back to the car at 12.40 a.m. after an exhilarating walk.

27 June 1965 I was now feeling rather tired so I drove to Loch Fyne and stretched out in my sleeping bag on the shore to get some sleep. Swarms of midges and showers of rain kept me awake so I rose at 4.30 a.m. and drove round to Rowardennan. At 6.45 a.m. I started up the tourist path on Ben Lomond, but the marshy path low down was disappointing. I enjoyed the ridge at the top and the solitude of the early morning, although long before I reached Rowardennan at 10.30 a.m. parties of walkers passed me going up the path.

I had crammed five Munros into the last 24 hours so I called it a day and drove slowly home.

Index

Achaladair, Beinn, 172 90
Aighenan, Beinn nan, 161
Alasdair, Sgurr, 99
Alder, Ben, 121 24
Alligin, Beinn, 62
Aonach Air Chrith, 82
Aonach Beag (Alder), 121 t 38
Aonach Beag (Lochaber), 115 38 6
✓Aonach Meadhoin, 78 129
Aonach Mor, 115 8
✓Aosda, Carn, 155 270
Attow, Ben – Beinn Fhada, 75
Avon, Ben, 126 16

Ballach, Carn, 106
Ban, Carn, 106
Ban Mor, Carn, 126
Ban, Sgurr, 42
Ban, Stob (Glen Nevis), 112
Ban, Stob (Loch Treig), 115
✓Banachdich, Sgurr na, 99 186
Basteir, Am, 99
Bhac, Carn, 155
✓Bhealaich Dheirg, Sgurr a', 78 91
Bheoil, Beinn, 121
Bhoidheach, Carn a'Choire – White Mounth, 150
Bhreac, Beinn, 137
Bhrotain, Beinn, 136 18
Bhuidhe, Beinn, 186
Bhuidheanach Bheag, A', 144
Bhuird, Beinn a', 126 10
Bhuiridh, Meall a', 162 43
Bidean nam Bian, 31 23
Bidein a' Choire Sheasgaich, 65
Binnein Beag, 113
Binnein Mor, 112 30
Blaven, 99
Bodach, Am, 112 95
Braeriach, 140 3
Braigh Coire Chruinn-bhalgain, 146 63
Breac, Sgurr, 55
✓Broad Cairn, 149 139
✓Bruach na Frithe, 99 198
Buachaille Etive Beag, 159
Buachaille Etive Mor, 158
Buidhe, Meall (Glen Lyon), 175
Buidhe, Meall (Loch Nevis), 88
Bynack More, 143 82

Caim, Carn na, 144
✓Cairn Bannoch, 150 114
Cairngorm, 140 5
✓Cairn of Claise, 152 63
✓Cairn Toul, 126 4
✓Cairnwell, The, 155 242
Caisteal, An, 184
Ceannaichean, Sgurr nan, 58
Ceapraichean, Meall nan, 35
Ceathreamhnan, Sgurr nan, 68 21
Chabhair, Beinn, 184
Chailleach, A' (Fannichs), 55
Chailleach, A' (Monadh Liath), 106
Challum, Beinn, 177
Chaorachain, Sgurr a', 65 74
Chaorainn, Beinn a' (Cairngorms),137 58
✓Chaorainn, Beinn a' (Craig Meagaidh), 110 76
Chlachair, Beinn a', 120 53
Chlaidheimh, Beinn a', 50
Chlamain, Carn a', 146
Chleibh, Beinn a', 169 273
Chno Dearg, 118 81
✓Chochuill, Beinn a', 164 168
Choinneach, A', 143
Choinnich, Sgurr, 65
Choinnich Mor, Sgurr, 115 50
✓Choire Bhoidheach, Carn a' – White Mounth, 15 33
Choire Ghairbh, Sron a', 87 236
Choire Ghlais, Sgurr a', 65 56
Choire Leith, Meall a', 180
✓Choire Odhair, Stob a', 162 224
Chonzie, Ben, 174
Chralaig, A', 75 32
Chrasgaidh, Meall a', 55
Chreachain, Beinn a', 172 59
Chroin, Beinn a', 184
Chuaich, Meall, 144
Ciche, Sgurr na, 88 88
Ciste Dhubh, 79
Ciste Duibhe, Sgurr na, 78
Clach Geala, Sgurr nan, 55 51
Clach Leathad – Clachlet, 162 Creise 48
Clachlet – Clach Leathad, 162
Cloich – mhuillin, Carn, 136
Coileachan, An, 55
Coireachan, Sgurr nan (Glen Dessarry), 88

✓ indicates I have done it. (Only ticked once if two entries on index)

✓ 1	Ben Nevis	1334 m
✓ 2	Ben MacDui	1309
3		
✓ 4	Carn Toul	1291
✓ 5	Cairngorm	1245
6		
✓ 7	Carn Mor Dearg 4000 ft	1223
8		
✓ 9	Ben Lawers	1214
10		
11		
12		
13		
14		
✓ 15	Ben More, Crianlarich	1174
16		
17		
18		
✓ 19	Lochnagar	1155
✓ 20	Derry Cairngorm	1155
21		
22		
23		
24		
25		
✓ 26	Craig Meagaidh	1130
✓ 27	Ben Lui	1130
28		
29		
30		
✓ 31	Ben Cruachan	1126
32		
✓ 33	Cairn a Choire Bhoidheach	1118
34		
35		
36		
37		
38		
39		
40		

41		
42		
43		
44		
✓ 45	Ben Ghlas	1103
46		
47		
48		
49		
50		
51		
52		
53		
54	_ _ _ _ _ _ (Snowdon)	
55		
56		
57		
58		
59		
60		
61		
62		
63		
64		
✓ 65	Meall Coranaich	1069
66		
✓ 67	Glas Maol	1068
✓ 68	Cairn of Claise	1064
✓ 69	Bidean a ghas Thuil	1062
✓ 70	Sgur Fiona	1059
71		
72		
73		
74		
75		
76	Ben a Chaorvinian	1052
77		
78		
79		
✓ 80	Carn an't Saggart Mor	1047

81	121
82	122
83	123
84	124
85	125
✓86 Meall nan Tarmachan 1043	126
87	✓127 The Devil's Point 1004
88	128
89	✓129 Aonach Meadhoin 1003
90	130
✓91 Sgurr a' Bhealaich Dheirg 1038	131
92	132
93	134
94	135
95	136
96	137
97	138
98	✓139 Broad Cairn 998
99	✓140 Ben More Assynt
100	✓141 Stob Diamh 998
101	142
102	143
103	144
104	145
105	146
106	147
107	148
108	149
109	150
110	151
111	
✓112 Carn an Tuirc 1019	✓152 Beinn Eunaich 989
113	153
✓114 Cairn Bannoch 1012	✓154 Conival 987
115	155
116	156
117	✓157 Creag Leacach 987
118	158
119	159
120	160

✓161	Ben Vorlich 985	201	
162		202	
163		203	
164		204	
165		✓205	Beinn Mhanach 954
166		206	
167		207	
✓168	Beinn a Chochuill 980	✓208	Meall Dearg (Aonach Eagach) 953
169		209	
170		210	
171		211	
172		212	
173		✓213	Driesh 947
✓174	Stob Choire Sgriodain 976	✓214	Creag a' Mhaim 947
175		215	
176		216	
✓177	Carn a Ghlasgoidh 975	217	
178		218	
✓179	Ben Lomond 974	219	
180		220	
181		✓221	An Socach 944
182		222	
✓183	Aonach Eagach - Sgorr nam Fiannaidh 967	✓224	Stob a' Choire Odhair 943
184		225	
✓185	Ben More, Mull 966	226	
✓186	Sgurr na Banachdich 965	227	
187		228	
188		✓229	Mount Keen 939
189		230	
190		231	
191		232	
192		233	
193		234	
		235	
✓194	Saileag 959	✓236	Sron a' Choire Ghairbh 935
195		237	
196		238	
✓197	Bruach na Frithe 958	239	
✓198	Tolmount 958	240	
✓199	Tom Buidhe 957		
200			